Praise for *The Measure of a Man*:

'Poitier's book is a fascinating read, as it offers much more than a glimpse of a man's life – you get a look at his soul . . . Poitier's chosen title for the book is incredibly fitting. Reading it you can almost hear him speak, measuring the weight and impact of his words'
Pride

'This remarkable book is not your conventional Hollywood biography. It is rather a memoir, a recollection, by an American icon of some of the key moments of his life . . . Poitier's conversational tone makes this a very intimate account of a memorable life. A delight'
Glasgow Times on Saturday

'*The Measure of a Man* isn't an anecdotal trawl through the film world; it's an opportunity for a morally aware individual to question himself and society . . . There is wisdom aplenty, because despite the racism he faced throughout his life, Poitier never channelled his anger into destructive force. His human dignity rests on every page'
Total Film

'Fascinating . . . this is a complex investigation of a complicated life. No punches are pulled and, at the end, I felt I knew the man. I couldn't ask for more'
Aberdeen Press and Journal

'A beautifully written and often humorous book – Poitier's passionate struggle against adversity will be an inspiration for anyone'
Manchester Metro

'This book is a personal history, trying to give contours to a full life in which Hollywood played only a part, albeit a major one. Unlike many stars, Poitier is able to discuss thoughtfully the values of his film work'
Boston Globe

'The dignified and elegant Poitier has a surprising side . . the rollicking

THE MEASURE OF A MAN

a memoir

Sidney Poitier

**POCKET
BOOKS**

LONDON • SYDNEY • NEW YORK • TORONTO

First published in Great Britain by Simon & Schuster UK Ltd, 2000
This edition first published by Pocket Books, 2001
An imprint of Simon & Schuster UK Ltd
A CBS COMPANY

3 5 7 9 10 8 6 4

Simon & Schuster UK Ltd
Africa House
64-78 Kingsway
London WC2B 6AH

Simon & Schuster Australia
Sydney

A CIP catalogue record for this book is available from the British Library

ISBN 13: 978-0-7434-0386-3

Printed and bound in Great Britain by
Cox & Wyman Ltd, Reading, Berks

To my wife, Joanna Shimkus-Poitier,
whose love and support has
kept me steady in the wind.

CONTENTS

Contents

ACKNOWLEDGMENTS

When I learned that Diane Gedymin at HarperSanFrancisco had expressed interest in my writing, I was thrilled and rushed to the assumption that she was drawn by something she read in the first set of rough and unorganized pages that outlined a book about the life I had lived. Perhaps fragments of how that life was lived caught her eye. Later, after getting to know her, I would think perhaps not. Perhaps she merely saw what her trained eye has come to accept as the familiar in the human condition. Perhaps she was a fearless observer of the endless variety of patterns that characterize human behavior. Maybe something like that accounts for the fact that her faith in this work registered early and remained so steadfast. In any case, all I know for sure is that without her enthusiasm, her support, and her guidance, this book would not have happened. My thanks to her for staying the course.

Liz Perle, also at HarperSanFrancisco, rendered service beyond the call of duty. She encouraged me to toil at the very edge of my limits and then challenged me to reach beyond. With her tirelessly urging me on, I almost never came up empty. I was fortunate to have Diane and Liz watching my back.

In *The Measure of a Man*, I tried to set my life down on the pages of this book as close as possible to the way it has been lived—without undue emphasis or understatement. When I finished writing, a series of serendipitous occurrences brought my editor, William Patrick, and my manuscript together—a most fortunate turn of events for my book and for me. Bill's talent runs deep and wide. To my delight, the man and his many gifts were no less than magical in their contributions. His professionalism and keen sense of the power of simplicity were absolutely indispensable in organizing, shaping, and focusing the material for this book. In his bones, William Patrick knows about writing, about books, about English language and literature. If I ever write another book, I hope that William Patrick will come back once more to work the magic in his bones.

I owe a debt of gratitude to my assistant, Susan Garrison, for getting me through the day, year after year without once falling on my face, even under the pressure of our perpetually inflexible schedule. I couldn't have gotten the work done in the fashion that I did without her special contributions. I am grateful that her hands were in the details.

The knowledge housed in the mind of my friend Charley Blackwell is awesome, whether it is book-learned, experience-gathered, or simply passed on from ancestors long gone. Hard-fought debates, won and lost, littered the space around our friendship—a reminder that we each tried our utmost to be, for the sake of the other, a worthy opponent. Traces of his life and thought can easily be seen on even the briefest journey across the pages of this book.

INTRODUCTION

MANY YEARS AGO I wrote a book about my life, which was, necessarily, in large part a book about my life in Hollywood. More recently I decided that I wanted to write a book about *life*. Just life itself. What I've learned by living more than seventy years of it. What I absorbed through my early experiences in a certain time and place, and what I absorbed, certainly without knowing it, through the blood of my parents, and through the blood of their parents before them.

I felt called to write about certain values, such as integrity and commitment, faith and forgiveness, about the virtues of simplicity, about the difference between "amusing ourselves to death" and finding meaningful pleasures—even joy. But I have no wish to play the pontificating fool, pretending that I've suddenly come up with the answers to all life's questions. Quite the contrary, I began this book as an exploration, an exercise in self-questioning. In other words, I wanted to find out, as I looked back at a long and complicated life, with many twists and turns, how well I've done at measuring up to the values I espouse, the standards I myself have set.

Writers of a spiritual or metaphysical persuasion often convey their message through storytelling. They illustrate their points with parables drawn from great teachers of the past, whether it be Jesus of Nazareth, or Buddha, or the latest Arabic sage or Sufi mystic—the more exotic the better. Some take this natural tendency to great lengths, writing whole books devoted to finding the deep wisdom embedded in ancient folk tales, psychologically complex stories drawn from Africa, Scandinavia, East Asia, Latin America, and many other far-flung countries. They do this, it seems, to get as far away as possible from our contemporary mindset so that we can see modern, digitized, postindustrial life as if through new eyes (or, perhaps, through very ancient, very grounded eyes).

For me the task is much easier. First of all, I've spent a very long time working in the dream factory called Hollywood. It's been my privilege—but also my daily business—to participate in constructing and dramatizing what those of us involved always hoped were meaningful stories, and putting them on the screen. Because I've always believed that my work should convey my personal values, as an author I don't have to look far to find storylines to illustrate points I wish to make. Happily, certain films that are a part of my own personal résumé are also part of the "collective unconscious" of a great many Americans of a certain age. It's my great good fortune that many of these films—stories such as *Lilies of the Field, A Patch of Blue, Guess Who's Coming to Dinner,* and *To Sir, with Love*—are still familiar today, thanks to home video and repeated play on television. Thus they give you and me the possibility of a common bond and a common frame of reference, and I want to use them that way.

But perhaps more important, as someone wishing to make a comment or two about contemporary life and values, I don't have to dig through libraries or travel to exotic lands to arrive at a view of our modern situation refracted through the lens of the preindustrial world, or the uncommercialized, unfranchised, perhaps even unsanitized—and therefore supposedly more "authentic"—perspective of the Third World. Very simply, this is because that "other" world, as alien as if separated by centuries in time, is the one from which I came.

THE MEASURE OF A MAN

ONE

THE IDYLL

IT'S LATE AT NIGHT as I lie in bed in the blue glow of the television set. I have the clicker in my hand, the remote control, and I go from 1 to 97, scrolling through the channels. I find nothing that warrants my attention, nothing that amuses me, so I scroll up again, channel by channel, from bottom to top. But already I've given it the honor of going from 1 to 97, and already I've found nothing. This vast, sophisticated technology and . . . nothing. It's given me not one smidgen of pleasure. It's informed me of nothing beyond my own ignorance and my own frailties.

But then I have the audacity to go *up again!* And what do I find? Nothing, of course. So at last, filled with loathing and self-disgust, I punch the damn TV off and throw the clicker across the room, muttering to myself, "What am I doing with my time?"

It's not as if I'm without other resources or material comforts, you follow? I've been very fortunate in life, and as I lie in my bed, I'm surrounded by beautiful things. Treasured books and art objects, photographs and mementos, lovely gardens on the balcony. After many years in this particular business in this particular town, I have a rich network of friends, some only a few steps away, dozens of others whom I could reach on the phone within seconds.

So what am I doing with my time?

Steeped in this foul, self-critical mood I lie back and close my eyes, trying to empty my head of all thought. It's late, time to sleep, so I determine to focus on that empty space in my consciousness and try to drift off. But images begin to come to me, infiltrating that darkness. Soft, sensuous images of a time very early in my life when things were so much simpler, when my options for entertainment couldn't be counted on a scale from 1 to 97.

I'M ON THE PORCH of our little house on Cat Island in the Bahamas. It's the end of the day and evening is coming on, turning the sky and the sea to the west of us a bright burnt orange, and the sky and the sea to the east of us a cool blue that deepens to purple and then to black. In the gathering darkness, in the coolness of our porch, my mother and father sit and fan the smoke from green palm leaves they're burning to shoo away the mosquitoes and the sand flies. And as she did so often when I was small, my sister Teddy takes me in her arms to rock me to sleep. While she's rocking me in her arms, she too is fanning the smoke that comes from the big pot of green leaves being burned, and she fans the smoke around me as I try to go to sleep in her arms.

That's the way the evenings always were on Cat Island. In the simplicity of that setting I always knew how I was going to get through the day and how Mom and Dad were going to get through the day and how, at the end of it, we were all going to sit on this porch, fanning the smoke of the burning green leaves.

On that tiny spit of land they call Cat Island, life was indeed very simple, and decidedly preindustrial. Our cultural "authenticity" extended to having neither plumbing nor electricity, and we didn't have much in the way of schooling or jobs, either. In a word, we were poor, but poverty there was very different from poverty in a modern place characterized by concrete. It's not romanticizing the past to state that poverty on Cat Island didn't preclude gorgeous beaches and a climate like heaven, cocoa plum trees and sea grapes and cassavas growing in the forest, and bananas growing wild.

Cat Island is forty-six miles long and three miles wide, and even as a small child I was free to roam anywhere. I climbed trees by myself at four and five years old and six and seven years old. I would get attacked by wasps, and I would go home with both eyes closed from having been stung on the face over and over. I would be crying and hollering and screaming and petrified, and my mom would take me and treat me with bush medicines from the old culture that you wouldn't believe, and then I would venture back out and go down to the water and fish alone.

I would even go in sometimes and swim by myself. I had the confidence, because when I was very small my mother threw me in the ocean and watched without moving as I struggled to survive. She watched as I screamed, yelled, gulped, and flailed in a panic-stricken effort to stay afloat. She watched as I clawed desperately at the water, unable to manage more than a few seconds before starting to sink beneath the surface. She watched as the ocean swallowed me, second by second. Then, mercifully, my father's hands reached under, fished me out, and handed me back up to my mother . . . who threw me back in again, and again and again, until she was convinced that I knew how to swim.

There were snakes on the island, but none poisonous. There were black widow spiders that were poisonous, but I doubt that my parents were fearful I would get killed by any of them. I mean, there were risks and there were hazards, but I could go anywhere, and I had myself as company.

I knew from observation that the sapodilla tree produced fruit, plump, grayish brown, soft, juicy, and delectable, at least twice a year, and that's where the wasps' nests were that got me unexpectedly and repeatedly. I learned early that if I got up high in a sapodilla tree, rather than crawling out on limbs to see if the fruit was ripe enough to eat, I could rattle the top branches of the tree and ripe fruit would come loose from the weakened stems and fall to the ground. And then I could come down and pick it up and eat and get my stomach full. I would eat until I got a bellyache, and then I would get more of my mother's bush medicine—god-awful-tasting grass weeds or bitter roots of plants whose names I've never known or chunks of aloe vera I would have to force myself to swallow. And then I was off again looking for cocoa plums. Or standing on the rocks by the sea and fishing with a piece of thread and a straight pin that I'd bent into a hook. I did all those things, and it was fun, because on such an island poverty wasn't the depressing, soul-destroying force that it can be under other conditions.

But the special beauty of Cat Island wasn't just what we had; it was also what we didn't have. Poverty notwithstanding, I was lucky, and the reason I was lucky was that I wasn't bombarded with contravening images and influences that really didn't have any direct connection to my nurturing. I didn't have to digest television—children's shows and cartoons. I didn't have to digest the stuff on radio and have to ask, "What are they saying? They're talking about selling me something. Why are they selling me something? I don't have a job." I didn't even have to deal with the myriad stimulations that come from the presence of mechanized vehicles. No one on the island had so much as a car or motorboat.

Now, if you take children in the modern United States that you and I are living in, they probably have a mom and a dad (or at least *one* parent), a set of grandparents possibly, and some siblings. But they're also going to have a radio in the house, and they're going to have a telephone (or at least know that such a thing exists), and they're going to know that there are television sets, and they're going to see people on the television sets who speak just like their mom and dad speak.

And they're going to be familiar with motion pictures too, because they'll start going when they're five or six. They're going to see talking animals moving around like people. They're going to see animals beating up on each other and slapping each other and falling down in crevices and getting up without experiencing intense pain. Some of these animals are then going to turn around and sell them breakfast cereal. These kinds of stimulations come at today's American kids on a daily basis, but the mental and emotional apparatus for sifting through them, for processing them, for dealing with them in some meaningful way, simply isn't there.

But children still have to try to make some sense of everything they're bombarded with. They have to assume *something*, correctly or incorrectly, factual or otherwise. They have to encode all these distractions into the self that they're slowly, day by day, building. Child psychologists have demonstrated that our minds are actually *constructed* by these thousands of tiny interactions during the first few years of life. We aren't just what's directed by our genes, and we certainly aren't just what we're taught. It's what we *experience* during those early years—a smile here, a jarring sound there—that creates the pathways and connections of the brain. We put our kids to fifteen years of quick-cut advertising, passive television watching, and sadistic video games, and we expect to see emerge a new generation of calm, compassionate, and engaged human beings?

In the kind of place where I grew up, what's coming at you is the sound of the sea and the smell of the wind and your mama's voice and the voice of your dad and the craziness of your brothers and sisters—and that's it. That's what you're dealing with when you're too young to really be counted into anything, when you're just listening, when you're watching the behavior of your siblings and of your mom and dad, noting how they behave and how they attend to your feedings and how they care for you when you have a pain or when the wasp stings you around your eye. What occurs when something goes wrong is that someone reaches out, someone soothes, someone protects. And as the people around you talk, you begin to recognize things that are carried on the voice. Words and behavior begin to spell out something to you. All those subtleties are what's going on with you, and that's *all* that's going on with you, day in and day out.

The rain comes and you hear the sound of it on the thatched roof and you sit waiting for it to stop because you want to go outside and play marbles—that is, play with the dried seeds from the pods of certain trees that were the marbles of my day. And if it's a Sunday, you want your mother to be able to get to the kitchen and cook the rice, because you know that you always have rice on Sunday. It's very simple, the exposure to the stimuli; and the stimuli are fairly natural ones, you understand? Fairly natural stimuli coming out of this family moving from the morning to night, to bedtime, to sleep, and they get up and move from morning to night again. They work in the fields growing tomatoes. (That's what my parents did when I was young; they were tomato farmers.)

Sometimes someone comes by with fresh fish that your parents can't put in the refrigerator because there's no such item. There's no freezer, either; there isn't even electricity! So what do they do? They clean the fish, pack it in salt, and hang it in the sun so that it cures and dries to a consistency as stiff as boards of wood. And it stays there for months and months and months, hanging in the kitchen on a line, and when your mother needs to cook that fish, she puts it in water and soaks it, and then she puts it in a pot and cooks it, and it's as terrific as ever it was when it was fresh.

On Cat Island I was stimulated, but I wasn't bombarded. I knew how I was going to get through the day, and how Mom and Dad were going to get through the day, and how we were all going to sit on the porch at the end of the day, together, fanning the smoke from the pot of burning green leaves to shoo away the mosquitoes and the sand flies.

THERE WASN'T A PAVED road on Cat Island. There wasn't a telephone on Cat Island. There were no stores except for a few petty shops, so my clothes were made out of the cloth of grain sacks. But Cat Island had plenty of paths. You walked pathways—trails that were there just because people had chosen a particular route as the quickest way for them to get from point A to point B. But most pathways were no more than maybe three or four feet wide. On either side of the three or four feet things grew wild. There were weeds, yes, and bushes and trees, but flowers were almost everywhere, and they bloomed like crazy. There were summer flowers, and flowers that responded to the weather, to the temperature, and many, like the sapodilla, that were in the habit of blooming several times a year.

So for the first ten years of my life, the years before tomato farming failed and we moved to Nassau, I had the responsibility, to a large extent, of taking care of myself. Things like being stung by wasps unexpectedly even when I thought I was smart enough to dodge them or get to the fruit without disturbing the nest—and I was wrong many times!—helped me to figure out some things about survival. Now, I'm talking about six, seven years old. When I got to a place where there was danger of one kind or another, I had to make a choice. Once I knew, or sensed, that there was danger of one kind or another, I had to determine, What's the wisdom of proceeding? Do I withdraw, do I try to go around?

There were times when I went near rock formations at the edge of the ocean where there were high cliffs along a road on the front part of the island, and I wasn't told, but I knew by just figuring it out, that if I fell over there, there was no way to climb back, and so how would I manage? I was smart enough by then to know that I would have to swim, but where could I swim to? Where could I manage to climb up? When I walked past this place where the rocks were high, this place where I would have no chance of recovering if I jumped in or fell in the water, I knew how far I would have to swim, and I knew damn well that I couldn't make that much distance swimming. So what did I do?

I chose to stay as far away from that edge as I could. I didn't need instructions or rules for that. I had a highly sharpened instinct for survival, refined by thousands of interactions with my environment.

On the other hand, I had an irresistible boyhood fascination with the dark mysteries hidden behind the things I didn't understand. In the village of Arthur's Town on Cat Island, there was a ditch one hundred feet long, six feet deep, dug from the sea to an inland salt pond. When a hand-hewn wooden trap was lifted, ocean water rushed through this ditch into the inland lake, where it evaporated into salt for the use of the island's inhabitants. Since it had been dug across the roadway that ran parallel with the waterfront, the ditch was covered over with wood. Six feet deep, at the most two feet wide, the awesome, dark, claustrophobic aspect of this ditch was enough to scare away most of the children on the island. We were all regaled with stories about its properties as a death trap. But I found this ditch just up my alley, so to speak. It was my Mount Everest, and I planned to conquer it.

One afternoon I entered this tunnel at the salt pond end and was swallowed up by darkness as I moved toward the trap door that kept the ocean out. About twenty-five feet in, as I was beginning to get deliciously scared, I discovered that the walls were narrowing, inch by inch, and that the water was getting deeper. A little farther on and I realized that I couldn't turn around. If I had to retreat, I would have to back out. But how fast could I move backward if the trap door gave way and sent the ocean rushing at me at fifty miles an hour?

With the images of moray eels, sea urchins, and other spiny creatures flooding my mind, I edged toward the trap door. At sixty feet in, the water was too deep for me to continue crawling, so I stood up and began to wade the rest of the way. At ninety feet in, the darkness was complete. The water was up to my neck, and I was scared shitless! Too scared to back up, I was also too petrified to press on.

Then I heard someone walking overhead across the wooden covering. I started to call for help but changed my mind when I thought about the whipping in store for me if my father learned about this adventure.

A moment later, whoever had been up there was gone, moved out of hearing range. While I stood there, passionately regretting having undertaken this incredibly dumb thing, I became aware of the sound of the water hissing through cracks in the trap door, and I realized that I was fairly close. Another ten feet and I would be home. Or another ten feet and I would be finished, depending on whether the tide was high enough to come rushing in or low enough to allow me to swim through to the rocks beyond. One way or another, I would know as soon as I reached that trap door and sprang it open.

I inched along on tiptoes as the water grew deeper, and finally I arrived at the door and the moment of truth. I reached up with both hands and yanked on the wooden trip-latch. Nothing happened. That "oh shit" feeling grabbed hold of me, and I yanked again and again and again—and nothing. I didn't have the strength. I was simply too small to put enough pressure on the lever to trip the latch and open the door.

This was as scared as I had ever been in my life up to that time. I started to cry and call for Mama. Dear Mama, she certainly would save me. I hollered for Mama—and I hollered and I hollered and I hollered. But to no avail. The only choice left open to me was to slowly retrace my steps. Too afraid even to try turning around, I began to inch my way backward the entire hundred feet out of the ditch.

That journey back was worse than the one before—nightmarish, terrifying—but I made it and quickly scurried out and up across the main road and down to the water's edge to check the tide. It was high—meaning that if I'd been able to open that trap door, my little ass would have been done for, swept at fifty miles an hour into the salt pond and buried there.

I was scared so badly by that experience, it was a week before I tried it again. But this time I checked on the tide, to make sure it wouldn't be running against me.

By the age of ten and a half, when I got to Nassau—which is the capital of the Bahamas and a real city—I had done much such flirting with risk, and much thinking for myself. Sometimes I was right; sometimes I was wrong—and every time I was right it strengthened something in me. By the time I reached Miami, Florida, at fifteen, entering the modern world as an immigrant teenager, I was still a kid, and I was still thinking like a kid, but I had something inside that was looking out for me. I had an inner eye that watched the terrain and watched the circumstances, especially when I was in hostile territory. This was my education, my Cat Island curriculum.

This watchful way extended to human nature—words, motivations, actions, and consequences. The quiet and simple atmosphere of my childhood enabled me to focus down to the level of the subtle body language that came at me from my parents and my siblings. On that tiny island I had gotten to know these signals really, really well. I had learned to read them just as I had learned to read the cliffs and the tides. I didn't understand them all, but over time I could use them as a reference point in trying to understand what others were saying, what they were doing, why they were behaving toward me as they were. I think that this is the basis for what has come to be called "emotional intelligence." It's a capacity that's nurtured by silence and by intimacy, and by the freedom to roam.

My mother, Evelyn, was a creature of silence. She was so inarticulate that she could hardly talk to anyone except my father. She couldn't speak to me much, though she communicated very eloquently in the way that she cared for me, the way her spirit hovers over me to this day, her presence always around me, guiding me in ways I'm still trying to understand.

My mother used to take me with her into the woods, to ponds where she would do her washing. These were the days before such things as washing machines, and we had no running water in the house, no electricity in the house. So when she washed clothing—and she washed the clothing for everyone in the family—she used to take it all in a big bundle into the woods, where rainwater settled into ponds. The ponds were like part of the marsh, but it would be fresh water—water you could wash clothing in. There used to be a soap called Octagon that came in an eight-sided bar, and she used to use that to get to the dirt in the clothing. Some people who had a few bucks, they had a scrub board, but she didn't. She would just beat the clothing on the rock until the dirt would sort of dissolve and float out. This water wasn't hot, mind you; it was cold water. And then she would wring the water out of each item and spread the clothes out on low trees to dry in the sun. We would be gone most of the day on those days when she washed, and when the clothes were almost dry, she would bundle them up and we would go back home.

These were the times when she would try to talk to me, and I never gave it a thought. She was just a mother. But the question arose later in my life and has persisted with me to this day. Who *was* this person?

Even up to the day I left her to go to Florida at age fifteen, I didn't really understand who she was, and here the dark side of me entered in. Shortly before I left, I said to her that when I got to America I wasn't going to write to her or send her any money. That was the most hurtful thing I could say, because by long tradition in the Bahamas, that's simply *what you did* when you went to America. You always sent back money. But hurting her is what I had set out to do, getting a little bit of revenge for something that she had done—what, I don't now recall. And separating, as teenage boys need to do.

But as I was leaving Nassau for good she did a fabulous thing. My older brother, who was in Florida, was working for some white people in Miami Beach. Occasionally he would get clothing handed down to him, and he would put it in a box and send it all to Nassau—you know, to the family. And once, in just such a box, came a shirt that my mother had set aside for me. It was a shirt that I wore infrequently because it was such a nice shirt. She thought it would be wonderful, since I was leaving, if she put new buttons on it. She put on these new buttons, and she buttoned my shirt and prepared to send me off.

I had never seen Mama as she was that day. In fact, she refused to go to the boat with me. She turned me over to my father, and we walked—I guess it was a good two and a half miles—to the dock, along the street on which I had spent so many of my young days. I felt such love as we walked, my love for the place and the people, and their love for me. People I knew, my friends, were all along the way, and we exchanged greetings. One particular friend was sitting on the fence of his parents' house, and my father stopped with me and gave me a few moments to spend with my friend. We said our goodbyes, and then I continued on with my dad to the dock. As I got on the boat, he said, "Take care of yourself, son," and that was that. He sent me off to Florida, and I wouldn't see my mother or my father again for eight years.

I believe that my mother was a very special human being, and I think that much that has happened to me is the continuance of her soul and her spirit and her gift. All that she was, all that she could never articulate, that she could never say to people . . . well, she felt far more than she could speak, and she lived, and she had children, and somehow the best of her found its way beyond her, beyond the bounds of her own life. I feel that whatever is good in me is that energy that she was. She put it into her last child. Does that make any sense to you?

I've always felt that my mother was this very pure and deserving entity, but on the level of my understanding as a youngster, she was just a mom, and she *was*; she was guilty of doing mom things—setting out restrictions and making demands and preventing me from making certain turns, life turns, I suppose. So when she talked to me on that level, she was a mom, from my point of view, talking to her son. Especially during some of the whippings she gave me—and there were quite a few, and they were all different from the whippings I got from my dad. My mother's discipline was emotional. When she would get to whipping on me, it was as if she could beat into me some wisdom that she knew would be essential for my survival.

I've told the story before, but I think it bears repeating here: the story of her concern at the time of my birth, and her going to the soothsayer. She was rightly concerned because I was a very premature baby, born unexpectedly while my parents were traveling to Miami to sell a hundred boxes of tomatoes at the Produce Exchange. When I arrived weighing in at less than three pounds, the question was, Is there enough there to take hold? My father, who had lost several children already to disease and stillbirth, was somewhat stoical about the situation. He went to a local undertaker in the "colored" section of Miami to prepare for my burial, coming home with a shoebox that could serve as a miniature casket.

My mother, however, felt that I could be saved. One afternoon she left the house where they were staying to visit the local palm-reader and diviner of tea leaves. After some intense gazing back and forth, and much silence, the soothsayer closed her eyes and took my mother's hand. There was more silence, an uncomfortably long silence, and then the soothsayer's face began to twitch. Her eyes rolled back and forth behind their lids. Strange sounds began to gurgle up from her throat. Then all at once her eyes flew open again and she said, "Don't worry about your son. He will survive and he will not be a sickly child. He will grow up to be . . . he will travel to most of the corners of the earth. He will walk with kings. He will be rich and famous. Your name will be carried all over the world. You must not worry about that child."

So for fifty cents, my mother found the support she needed for backing a long shot. She came home and ordered my father to remove the shoebox of a casket from the house—there would be no need for it. And so it followed, for reasons that my mother and I believed were better left unquestioned, that I pulled through.

I wasn't a spoiled child. As soon as I was big enough to lift a bucket, I carried water for my mother. I went into the woods to gather bramble to make our cooking fire. Even as a toddler I had my jobs, my purpose, and I knew that I had to contribute to the thin margin of our survival. But I was a child bathed in love and attention.

My mother wasn't my only guardian angel. One day my sister Teddy said to me, "What are you going to do? What would you like to do when you grow up?" And I remember—at that time I was about twelve—I told my sister that I would like to go to Hollywood and become a cowboy.

I had just seen my first movie—it was a cowboy movie, of course—and I thought it was the most amazing thing. I had no idea that Hollywood meant the movie business. I thought Hollywood was where they raised cows, and where they used horses to keep the cows corralled, and where the cowboys were the good guys, and they were always fighting the bad guys, who were trying to either steal the cows or do something to the people who owned the cows, and I wanted to do *that* kind of work.

Teddy laughed, but the laughter wasn't *at* me; she laughed *with* me. She was somebody who really loved me a lot, like my mom. She was more than ten years older, and she laughed. I'm sure she must have thought it was so wonderful that I was having this terrific dream, but she didn't correct me, she didn't say, "That's such a way-out fantasy." She didn't say, "Who do you think you are? Man, you better get your feet on the ground. Boy, you got a long way to go." No, she obviously had dreams too.

About ten years later the family was able to gather in a theater in Nassau to see the first picture I ever made, something called *No Way Out*. This was in 1950, and it was the first time my parents had ever seen a movie. It must have been something like a fantasy for them, a dream. I'm not entirely sure how much they grasped of the concept.

My mother was sitting there, a woman who really didn't

know anything about movies. My father was sitting there, a guy who really didn't know anything about movies. The movie played, and they were absolutely enthralled with what they saw, letting go with "That's my kid!" and all that. But near the end of the movie Richard Widmark pistol-whips me in the basement of some house. He's hitting me with this pistol, the butt of this pistol. He's beating the crap out of me with this pistol, and my mother jumps up in the theater and yells, "Hit him back, Sidney! Hit him back! You never did nothing to him!" In front of everybody. My brothers and sisters are squirming and laughing, saying, "Mama, sit down, sit down." But she's not joking. She's for real, completely in the moment. "Hit him back, Sidney! Hit him back!"

That was my mother.

———

THERE ARE THINGS that pass through us along the blood-line that don't surface in our children, or in our grandchildren. They may not even surface in our great-great-great-grandchildren, but eventually they will surface, you know?

If you walk down the street and someone is with you, he'll adjust to your pace or you to his, and you'll never be aware of it. There's no effort. It simply happens. And the same thing can happen with the rhythm of your life.

We're connected with everything. We're connected with the primal instincts. And whatever is primal in us goes to the beginning of the species and back even beyond that. You follow?

We carry a sensitivity panel, a panel of connected sensitivity remembrances all passed along through the blood, because if we're standing or sitting or lying somewhere alive at this moment, then we're living proof that our bloodline is unbroken from the beginning of time.

Now, a great prodigy like Mozart, when he can barely walk, finds a piano, and he goes over to this instrument, curious, looks it over, tinkers with it, hears some sounds, and in no time is able to begin to make sense of the notes that respond to his touch, and by the age of three he's writing symphonies. The music and the instrument simply speak to him. At an organic level he understands the harmonies and the chord structures. Even before he can read he's primed for what he's going to do in his life.

But where did that come from? Could it not have come from ten generations before him, when a child was born with this unbelievable gift but nobody knew it? It was just there, because nature doesn't place either a prize or a price on such gifts. It simply deposits them, and they can stay dormant in the bloodline for centuries. They don't necessarily have to be passed from father to son, you know?

So the primal thing is a very real part of our existence. How do I know that there wasn't a gift for theater or a gift for storytelling in my background two hundred years ago, four hundred years ago, seven hundred years ago? Maybe it lay dormant or was momentarily activated and returned to dormancy as it traveled along the bloodline generation after generation.

And one day, bingo! It's in a child who walks into a certain place, and certain circumstances, and suddenly it comes to life.

Now, that could go for musicians, it could go for scientists, it could go for the griots in the old days in Africa or the bards in Europe. That's the way it goes, because it's a single human family. The apparatus is the same.

All those experiences were registered, because there was a consciousness that was taking all that stuff in, even if it couldn't articulate it or define it. It was just taking that stuff in and responding. There was a response to it, just a nervous response, an instinctive response, and that was passed on, and the next generation got it in some form or other and the next generation after that in some form or other and all the way across history.

AS A MATTER OF FACT, it's hard to tell where I came from. Poitier obviously is a French name. Given that we were in an English colonial possession, and that Poitier in the Bahamas is associated only with black people, there's the strong implication that the bearers of that name came from Haiti, the nearest French colonial possession to the Bahamas. We have to assume that my ancestors escaped, because there's no record of a Poitier family of whites having gone to the Bahamas. So my people left on their own. The other French colonial possessions are way, way, way deep in the Caribbean, and to my mind it's unlikely that any black people would have migrated all the way across the Caribbean from Martinique, or St. Martin, or Guadeloupe into the Bahamas.

The speculation is that the family originated in Haiti and moved by escape routes to the Bahamas, settling eventually on Cat Island. Now mind you, the French in Haiti supported slavery, as did the British colonies, so at the time of my family's migration to the Bahamas, they weren't coming from a slave state to a free state. But Cat Island was such an isolated place that they probably had no difficulty in finding, if not a family to work for, then at least land that they could sharecrop and live on.

Cat Island had enormous land area relative to its population. I mean, it was forty-six miles long, with a population of maybe one or two hundred white families, you know? And maybe three or four hundred slaves. So we assume that my ancestors simply started farming, and if anybody bothered to say, "By the way, what are you doing on my land?" they would have said, in French or whatever, "We're just here," and then the owners would have said, "Okay, well, you know, this is my land, and you have to give me some of what you produce."

My grandfather, March Poitier, wasn't a farmer, though. He was very skilled at building. He would be contracted by the state, by the government, to go to other islands and build a schoolhouse or a government building or some other public structure. That required, first of all, having a boat, which in those days he would have had to build himself. It doesn't appear, according to the oral history of the family, to have been an enormous boat. Rather, it was probably one that took a sail stitched together from the sturdiest canvas cloth he could afford. He most likely made a mast out of a tree chopped down in the forest, skinned of bark and fastened in the bow. His rigging rope was either store-bought or handmade. If handmade, it was plaited from sisal, an inhospitable plant with thornlike edges running along the sides of its leaves and culminating at its end in a point as sharp as a needle. Put in water, the tough skin of the sisal leaf dissolves after some weeks, leaving a strong, stringy, threadlike material that's widely used by those in the rope-making business.

My later experience with boats as a young man leads me to say that his boat probably was a fifteen-footer. It couldn't have been more than an eighteen-footer. He made a sail because motors were out of the question. You didn't even talk about motors in those days, though he would probably have had a couple of oars.

In the Caribbean they row from the stern. He would have had a couple of oars, and he would have had a bailing bucket so that if he ran into difficult weather he could bail the water out of the boat.

Now, crucial to getting a fix on what his character might have been—the places he went to build these houses for the government, they weren't just around the corner. He would have had to sail great distances in open water. For instance, to go from Cat Island to the Exumas by motorboat doing ten, eleven knots an hour is a four-hour run. So if he was using sail or the oars, you're talking about at least an overnight run. In fact, you're talking about twenty to twenty-five hours or so, in open seas by himself!

It's my understanding that his job was to collect local people on-site that he would hire to do the job. He was a builder on Cat Island as well, but he was often gone, sometimes for months at a time. On one such trip he was bitten by a black widow spider and took sick on the return trip. By the time he arrived home, he was in very bad shape, and he died.

But March Poitier had a lot of sons and daughters. He had been married before he married my grandmother, with whom he had three children—David, Caroline, and Reggie.

Both grandparents on my father's side were dead before I was born. But on my mother's side I knew Pa Tim and Mama Gina. I knew them because they lived close to us on Cat Island, and they were wonderful but very old people who were still very much in the old culture.

My grandfather Pa Tim was a farmer, an extremely tall man who said few words but was very close to my grandmother. I remember her better. She smoked a pipe and cooked in a thatch hut, and her hair was always tied up with a cloth, like a handkerchief, as I recall, and she was very close to her children. She had five daughters: my mother, Evelyn, Eunice, Aida, Ya-Ya, and Augusta.

My grandmother lived just across the pond from our family. I remember my Aunt Ya-Ya, who died after I left for Florida, and I remember very well my Aunt Augusta, who also smoked a pipe—that same kind of white-clay pipe from the olden days.

There was something special in the women of that family. My mother had it, which made my father a very fortunate fellow. Ya-Ya I recall having had it too, but Auntie Gusta—it seems to me I saw most of it in Auntie Gusta.

Auntie Gusta left her husband, Zack, because he was abusive. He drank, and whenever he was able to scrounge up enough bucks he would shell it out on rum. He was a hardworking man, but he spent such monies as he could manage on rum (or he bartered goods, farm products, for rum), and he was an abuser. She only had the courage to leave him once the children were grown. She got on a boat and she went to Nassau and tried to find a new life for herself. Boy, you don't know how much courage that took. But that was my mother's family.

My mother had a marriage that was unbelievable, and I think it had to do simply with a compatibility that was native to the two personalities. They got along so well. I never heard a cross word. My mother could talk only to my dad—*really* talk—but they would talk and talk and talk. I mean, they were friends and they were buddies and they worked side by side. She respected him, and he—I think he might have been guilty of a few infractions here and there—was devoted to her and would never hurt her. Never, *never*. You see, he was some years older than Evelyn. Evelyn was thirteen when they got married. Reggie, then not quite twenty-six, was the only man she ever knew.

In 1936 the state of Florida imposed an embargo against tomatoes grown in the Bahamas. That turn of events would require thirty-two years to break down Reggie Poitier, and several more to wrestle the life out of him, but the struggle was set in motion mid-morning of a warm, sunny day in 1937, when my mother and I stepped on board a native sailboat.

Around us, my father, my older brothers and sisters, and my grandparents on my mother's side all stood or squatted on the jagged coral outcroppings that made the waterfront of Arthur's Town, Cat Island. Behind them, high on a bluff adjacent to the main road, a chorus of cousins, once or twice removed, milled about in a modest crowd of neighbors, friends, and assorted well-wishers. All had come to offer a prayer for our safe passage and wave us goodbye.

This was the first step in my father's plan to resettle the family. My mother and I were to travel to Nassau as an advance party "to take a look at the lay of the land," search out housing we could afford, and gather such additional information as would be relevant to our survival in an unfamiliar place. The second step, depending on a favorable report, would require the rest of the family to follow in the weeks to come. But on that morning I was a ten-and-a-half-year-old boy whose thoughts were far from the pressing realities of family survival. While I was old enough to pick up ever so slight changes in my father's face and something unspoken in his eyes, I was still far too young to read or even recognize concerns of obligation when written on a face. Instead, my thoughts roamed freely in a fantasy arena.

Weeks before departure time, my imagination had begun running wild with anticipation. When the moment to step on board finally arrived, I was almost *too* excited, *too* anxious, *too* filled with curiosity and wonder about what kind of world I would find beyond the horizon. From rumors, hearsay, and snatches of adult conversations never meant for my ears, I had concluded that whatever world I would find waiting for me must surely be like no place I had ever seen or dreamed of.

I had heard that there were real electric lights there, not kerosene lamps like the ones everybody on Cat Island used. Running water *inside* houses. Coming in through pipes from under the ground. With the twist of a little handle, water would come when you wanted. As much as you wanted, as little as you wanted. I had heard that sworn to as a fact. Yet how could that be? And more wild than that, "cars," they said, were a sight to behold. They said some people somewhere in that world beyond the horizon had made something called a car that would run faster than a horse—which was the fastest thing I knew of. Having never seen a car, I wondered how on earth they managed to make such a thing. And shoes. How about people who had shoes and wore them all the time? Not just on Sundays. Even toilets, they said, were found *inside* some rich people's houses. Couldn't imagine how *that* would work.

As those on shore waved and shouted their goodbyes, the anchor was hoisted, the sail was set, and our vessel eased out to sea.

First the waterfront of Arthur's Town grew smaller and smaller; then Cat Island itself became a dot on which I focused intently until it disappeared from sight. Looking back now, in my mind's eye, I remember it as a place where a simple people, three hundred families strong, managed their survival through an improvised, communal existence. Until the embargo, tomato farming was the closest thing to an industry that we had. On an island that consisted mostly of coral rock, each family could still find a plot of ground big enough to call a family farm, and fertile enough to meet a family's needs. Some who didn't work a farm built boats. Some built houses. Others were fishermen or well-diggers or shopkeepers.

At some time in the distant past a marriage had taken place between a barter system and a cash economy, and that marriage had endured into a benign tradition. Competition was kept as close to neighborly levels as was possible. The person who built houses would probably have to take some goat or fish meat in addition to some money for his services. For those who didn't have cash, an exchange of their labor served as a viable currency just as well. That way everything leveled out. Thatched-roof houses without plumbing were built largely from materials found around the island. Taxes? There were none. Therefore, a family could function from year to year having only the slightest amount of cash. No money was needed to build a rock oven for baking; the rocks were there in abundance. A family would build a lime kiln from freshly cut trees that were still green and burn them over many weeks until the green wood became an ash with a consistency resembling cement. It wasn't actually cement, but it had a texture that ultimately hardened like cement, allowing them to build the walls of a house. They could build a door out of wood and nails if they had those things. If not, they used twine to secure pieces of wood together to form a door. Protein came in the form of pigs, goats, chickens, and fish.

I was just a child when we left, and none of us were particularly given to introspection back then. But nearly sixty years later, a dear friend asked a very telling question. "On Cat Island," he asked me, "when you looked in the mirror, what did you think about the color of your skin?"

The question opened doors that helped me to understand that special place. I told him, first of all, that I had no recollection of having seen myself in a mirror at that time. I couldn't remember having ever seen a looking glass in our house, or any other kind of glass anywhere on the island (except maybe rum bottles on the shelf of Damite Farrah's shop). No glass windows, no glass doors, no stores with glass fronts. Our family didn't drink from glassware; we drank from enamel cups. Reflections, of course, from pond water, baking pans, various other kinds of metals. That's what I had. That's *all* I had. Occasional glimpses from reflections. Never was I able to recall having seen myself in a mirror. So I never got a fix on my color. No reason to. With no frame of reference to evidence its necessity, the issue never arose. There was one guy in Arthur's Town, a doctor, who was white, and Damite Farrah, the shopkeeper, who was white. These guys were different-looking, yes. But neither represented power. Therefore, I never translated their color into that. Or control . . . or hostility . . . or oppression . . . or anything of that nature. They were just there, and I never wondered why they were white and the rest of the people were black.

So in answer to my friend's question, I *didn't* think about the color of my skin. Not any more than I would have bothered to wonder why the sand was white or the sky was blue.

But outside the island of my early years, a world was waiting that would focus on my color to the exclusion of all else, never caring to go beyond that superficial characteristic to see what else I might have to offer. As I entered this world, I would leave behind the nurturing of my family and my home, but in another sense I would take their protection with me. The lessons I had learned, the feelings of groundedness and belonging that had been woven into my character there, would be my companions on the journey. But so too would those intimations of the dark side I had first glimpsed in myself, even in the idyllic setting of my childhood, that I didn't yet understand. As I moved on to live my life, fidelity and faithlessness, great good fortune and barely skirted annihilation, would flicker in and out of the script of my life. Always, lurking behind the objects and experiences of the everyday world, there were the mysteries. Why is there something instead of nothing? Why have I survived, even prospered? Is it all purely random and meaningless, or is there something more to be revealed?

TWO

DEPARTURES

WHEN I WENT BACK to the Bahamas to live in the seventies, I had a small boat, about a twenty-footer, that I used just for solitude. I would go cruising by myself quite a ways out from the eastern end of Nassau. One day, while fishing a few miles from a cluster of small, uninhabited islands, I got a big strike that felt like a good-size fish. I stood up in the boat to set the hook, and as I furiously started reeling the fish in, something happened—and it was gone.

I don't know whether the fish just got loose or a barracuda took it, but suddenly there I was, floundering, sulking over the loss of my fish, and the line was loose, drifting down into the water.

Because I was slow to react, the line sank to the bottom, and because I was over coral, which was maybe forty feet down, the hook got stuck. Still standing up in the boat, I figured I'd start the motor and back over the spot where my hook was wedged in and then pull it the other way. So I started the motor and was moving around, and as I was fussing with the line, trying to get it unhooked, the boat swaying this way and that, I suddenly realized that if I fell off that boat with the motor going, and going just fast enough so that there was no way I could catch it by swimming behind it—well, not to put too fine a point on it, if I fell out of that boat, I'd be done for. Bye-bye. All over.

I was maybe two and a half miles from the nearest island, in forty feet of open water. I could float, mind you. I could get on my back and float, but the tide would have to be ideal not to move me away, pull me out in the direction of the Gulf Stream even if I were paddling like the whole U.S. Olympic swim team rolled into one.

Once again I had yielded to the seduction of risk, only to recoil from the awful sense of vulnerability. No beautiful wife, no film credits, no lovely friends and dinner invitations, no money in the bank was going to save me if I fell into the drink. After that realization I never, ever moved around in the boat unless I was anchored, and I never, ever started the motor unless I was seated at the console. But it was hardly the last time I would dance close to the edge.

Nassau was my first exposure to the myriad risks that lay outside the natural world. Urban life was infinitely more than

I had expected, and it came at me with breakneck speed. Forming. Shaping. Molding. Seasoning a ten-and-a-half-year-old boy to bring him rapidly up to speed in a town where everything moved ten times faster than in the place he had left behind. Everything was new. Friends, values, social imprinting, transfer of allegiance from the old family of blood to the new family of friends.

At the age of ten and a half, I ran smack into Urban. Modern. Cars. Movies. Hotels. Restaurants. Night clubs. Bars. Dance halls. And that transition from childhood idyll to Urban launched me straight into manhood. By the age of fourteen I was no longer a child.

When childhood is aborted, it's like aborted grief. In both cases, if you don't go through all the stages, giving each its due, the job never gets completed. I felt that double thing: part of me said, "Yes—make the plans, do the decisions, take the responsibility, pull the load"; at the same time, I felt that there was a kid inside me who'd never got finished.

The pain I felt most sharply was the loss of camaraderie, the sense of belonging. I grieved for the love, the trust, and the feel-good giggles that had once bubbled up and bound me to the friends of my childhood, most of whom are dead now, and bound those childhood friends to me. Not that my life was all that bad.

Even these days the smile still comes when I think how we used to go to the movies in Nassau, then come back in the evening and act out all the parts. Then there was the time we stole a case of rum during a riot and climbed over the eight-foot wall of an old, run-down estate, settled in some bushes, and drank till we got pissed. Then found we couldn't climb back over the wall! Every day, with testosterone kicking ass, we would search out something crazy to do.

Whenever I could play games in those early days in Nassau . . . whenever I could run with buddies . . . go to a movie . . . hang with the fellas . . . do harmless but mischievous and, I suppose, childish things—that was my delight. I have great remembrances of long, long silences filled with the satisfaction, the pleasure of just being together doing nothing in particular. Or suddenly bursting into laughter from a remembered moment once shared. Laughing till I cried was a special kind of joy. Laughing so hard my stomach hurt.

I didn't have much of that for very long. All of it stopped before I could finish being a kid. But today the laughter of birds and the chatter of monkeys remind me that the source experiences that trigger delight in each of us are different. To each of us a certain kind, in each of us a certain amount. Nothing is transferable. One makes do with what one gets.

Plunked down so suddenly in the middle of that new world, I had to struggle to get a fix on myself. I ended up getting a look at me by looking at that new world. As I looked at the goods it had available, I could see myself reflected in the glass window showcases of all the stores I passed on Bay Street. I had to get a fix on the folks, too. Now there were white people all over the place. A hell of a lot more than the two at Arthur's Town, Cat Island.

When I first went to school in Nassau I attended Eastern Senior, which was a long way off from where we lived—a good four-mile walk one way. And four miles back. On the convoluted route I liked, because it appeared to be a shortcut, I ran into a white kid who was about my age. His name was Carl, and I would see him almost every day on my way *from* school or on my way *to* school. He seemed to be friendly enough, so one day I stopped to talk with him. In a couple of weeks we had struck up a loose friendship, exchanging thoughts of interest to our age and gender. I would learn from him by asking questions; he would respond, and in turn ask questions of me. In time we arrived at the question of race. He wasn't at all shy about letting me know that *he* was better off than I was, on the basis of his color. According to the gospel as he had learned it, I would never have the same opportunities, the same circumstance in life that he would.

I waited for the punchline. None came. He was dead serious! When I recovered from the shock, what he had said rankled the shit out of me. I responded with all the things I suppose a young black kid *would* say. You know the sort of thing. "I can do anything you can do. I can climb a tree as quickly as you. I can run as fast as you. I can do anything you can do, quicker and better."

But the more I protested, the more my words seemed to reinforce his matter-of-fact smugness. His whole manner indicated that this wasn't deluded opinion he was spouting; to him it was absolute truth. I kept pounding back until he got testy, and then we both pounded back some more. We went on like that for some time, shooting at each other the most hurtful things we could think of, only to wind up as eleven-year-old boys

35

tend to wind up: pissed, exhausted, and off on their separate ways to other concerns—until they see each other again, and then it's like nothing happened.

Three years later, in another part of Nassau, I met a girl named Dorothy. She was very fair complected, but you could see that there was some color there. She lived out near the water in a mixed neighborhood with her mother and a brother. When I met her I had pleasant feelings like butterflies in my stomach, and it appeared that she had the same. We started making eyes at each other and some magic happened. Then I met her brother—who turned out to be Carl. They were from two different fathers, Carl and his sister. The mother was white. And the father of Dorothy was a person of color.

So I suppose Carl was in a complicated situation emotionally. And I suppose that he felt better when his vanity could get a boost at the expense of mine. But his conflict was not unusual. In Nassau, race was still a slightly ambiguous issue.

For some people, though, there was no ambiguity. One day on West Bay Street, when I was walking past the old fort near the waterfront, I saw ahead of me an older white guy coming on a bicycle. Had to have been between eighteen and twenty, I'd say. I was walking along toward the west. Just the two of us on the street, you know? No cars or anything at that particular time. He was moving east on the left-hand side of the street when I noticed him starting to turn toward me. I figured he was heading around the upcoming corner. He rode up, and as he got abreast of me he took his right hand off his handlebar and punched me right in the face.

BOOM!

I was stunned. It took me a few seconds to pull myself together, and when I did, I saw him tearing ass a mile a minute toward the center of town. I took off after him. But he was heading downtown, and downtown was *owned* by white people. Of course, at age fourteen that made no difference to me.

He looked back and he saw me coming, running as hard and as fast as I could.

He ducked around a corner and onto Bay Street, which was the main business thoroughfare. By the time I arrived at the foot of the street and looked east, he had disappeared. Not a bicycle in sight.

I went into every store looking for him. I walked Bay Street, remembering what he looked like, remembering how he was dressed, and even *now* I can still see him. Clear as can be. He was dressed in bicycle gear, decked out as only a kid of some wealth could be.

After a good hour looking, I still hadn't found him.

Which was lucky for me. In retrospect, maybe one of the luckiest occurrences of my life. Considering my state of mind, had I found him, chances are I would have gone right at him. But with the full power of the state inevitably on his side, the satisfaction I sought would have come at a very high price.

Beyond these first tinges of racism, I also became aware of something else that I had never before come upon. Even though I had only the dimmest glimmer of an understanding of the concept of "class," it came to me in the form of a warning: "Here, not everybody is the same." I absorbed the message that there were ground rules I would be expected to observe. I saw quite quickly that the entire white population was an elite element when evaluated against the black population, but there was obviously an elite element even *within* the white population. And there was an elite element to the *black* population as well.

The black upper class was a good thing to see, but to me, it smelled like a warning as well. There were black businessmen. There were black school principals, black policemen, black judges, *and* black lawyers. The majority of the blacks, of course, were workaday poor, very poor. Poor in Nassau was like poor on Cat Island, only tougher, because survival in Nassau was more heavily dependent on money. In Nassau even some black folks had electricity, but we still used a kerosene lamp. Some had a bathroom in the house, and glassware dishes, even an icebox. For the first time I began to see myself against that reality. There were haves and have-nots, and we definitely had very little. We had no money, no power. We lived in the requisite neighborhood for *those* people.

I then knew what the pecking order in that part of the world was. Couldn't miss it. Plus, I knew where I was in *it*. For myself, it was okay, because my life was ahead of me. But I didn't like where my dad was in it. My father, an honorable fellow trying awfully hard, was at the very bottom of the pole. I remember one occasion distinctly. He was sitting on the porch near the door of the last house we lived in, before I left Nassau. As I barreled past him on my way out to hook up with friends, he reached out and stopped me. He looked me up and down.

He felt my arms. I must have appeared rather thin to him. He said, "You're not eating regularly, are you, son?" I said, "I'm okay. I'm all right. I'm fine." He didn't say more. I felt terrible for him because I knew what was going on in his head that he couldn't put in words. I loved him for it, you know?

My mother used to buy flour sacks and make pants and shirts for my school clothes. Seemingly endless fun was made of me because I wore the emblem of the flour company on my bottom. But knowing that my mom and dad were doing the best they could gave me the strength to suck it up and move on. Especially when Mom said, "Look, this is where we are now. There's no shame in what you wear as long as it's clean. Your father and me, we put clothes on your back as best we can. You just remember there are other colored people who have a lot more. So it's just a question of—well, maybe one day we'll do better; maybe one day we'll get there too. It's not impossible, son. It's not impossible."

But that environment didn't make it easy. By the age of thirteen I had dropped out of school, a short tenure, given that my formal education began around the age of eleven. At the age for junior-high sock-hops I was doing hard labor around construction jobs. My best friend, Yorick Rolle, was caught stealing a bicycle—an adventure I don't to this day know why I wasn't a part of—and he was sent off for four tough years in the colonial prison system. My brother Cedric, two years older than I, was sent away because of a bizarre extortion scheme that was fueled by a combination of adolescent naïveté and too many caper movies, I'm sure. And even I, little Sidney Poitier, was jailed briefly for stealing corn. So it wasn't a tough call for my father to say he had to get me out of there. I was sent off to live in Miami with my brother Cyril, more than ten years my senior.

———

MIAMI SHARED A CLIMATE and lifestyle with the Caribbean, but its culture and mores were of the American South, 1940s Jim Crow style, and nothing had prepared me to surrender my pride and self-regard sufficiently to accept those humiliations. In fact, it was quite the opposite. My values and my sense of self were already fully constructed.

Which is another way of saying that I was already a kid who wasn't gonna take any bullshit—from anybody.

While I was in no position to force society to accept me as I wanted to be accepted, I still had to let people know what *my* rules were. For a while I had a job as a delivery boy, and on one of my first assignments I was sent to a wealthy home in Miami Beach. I went to the front door and rang the bell, and a lady came to the door and said, "What do you want?"

"Good afternoon, ma'am," I said. "I've come to deliver your package from the drugstore."

"Get around to the back door where you belong," she snapped.

"But I'm *here*. Here's the package you ordered." I extended the bag containing her items.

She huffed and slammed the door in my face. I just couldn't understand what her problem was. I set the package down on the step in front of the door and left. I didn't think any more about it.

A couple of nights later, when I came home my brother's house was completely dark, and the family was lying on the floor, huddled together as if they were in a state of siege. It seems the Klan had been there looking for me, and everyone in the house was terrified. Everyone except me. Being new and from a different culture, I was wide-eyed with *curiosity*, mostly at the family's reaction. I just couldn't get used to this strange place and this strange way of behaving.

In Nassau, while learning about myself, I had become conscious of being pigeonholed by others, and I had determined then to always aim myself toward a slot of *my* choosing. There were too many images of what I could be. Where I could go. Too many images of wonderful, accomplished, interesting black people around and about for me to feel bad about my color.

In Miami, this strange new society started coming at me with point-blank force to hammer home its long-established, non-negotiable position on the color of skin, which declared me unworthy of human consideration, then ordered me to embrace the notion of my unworthiness. My reply was, "Who, me? Are you fucking crazy? *Me?* You're talking to me?"

I was saying, "Hey, not only am I *not* that which you would make me. Here's what I in fact *am*. First of all, I'm the son of a really terrific guy, Reginald James Poitier. And Evelyn Poitier, my mom, who's a terrific woman. I have no evil designs; I'm a well-intentioned, meaningful person. I'm young, and I'm not particularly headstrong—though I can get pretty pissed. I'm a good person, and nothing you say can undo that. You can harp on that color crap as much as you want, but because of the way I was raised, I don't have a receptor that's gonna take in any of that."

Of course, over time, osmosis brings a lot of that sewage to you, and some of it does seep in, you know? But having arrived in America with a foundation that had had time to set, the Jim Crow way of life had trouble overwhelming me.

Vanity, which the dictionary says is an excess of pride, was the only way I could brace myself against the onslaught of the culture's merciless indictment of me. With no other means at my disposal to fight off society's intent to restrict my range of motion, to smother and suffocate me, excess was engaged to speak on my behalf. I was saying, "Okay, listen, you think I'm so inconsequential? Then try *this* on for size. All those who see unworthiness when they look at me and are given thereby to denying me value—to you I say, 'I'm not talking about being *as good as* you. I hereby declare myself *better* than you.'"

Later, I would carry that theme, detached from questions of color and race, all the way into the theater world, where it would become a personal standard, applicable to creative excellence and professional competitiveness. Marlon Brando was an idol of mine, a consummate artist and one of the good guys. I aimed to be *better* than even him.

But I didn't need anyone to torture me or deny me or coddle me or cajole me into having that kind of drive. I was born with an innate curiosity, and it took me to the damnedest places.

When I was small the world was an Eden. I woke up in the morning saying, "I'm seven and I'm free! I can walk to the ocean and I can jump in. My brothers kick my ass now and then, but that's okay. There's all this newness! There's life! There's girls! There's that damned ditch that nearly got me killed. It's a whole world of fascinating challenges."

Natural threats laid the foundation, but there was always a who or a what or a condition challenging me to prove my value. Pushing, forcing, threatening me to be better. Always better. I was challenged to understand all the abuse in the world. When I got to Nassau, it was race and class and economics, a colonial system that was very hostile. So my motto was *Never leave home without a fixed commitment.* I couldn't deal with those awesome odds either by waiting for society to someday have a change of heart or by saying, "I'm gonna be as good, one day, as you are." My heart said, "I am already as good. In fact, I'm starting out with better material, and I am going to be better." How do you like *them* apples?

Young blacks coming up in America were frequently subjected to parental lectures, almost all of which carried the same message: "Face this reality. You're gonna have to be twice as good as the white folks in order to get half as much." That was drilled into them. Bahamian lectures had another ring. "Get that education. Get out there and work. Get out there and hustle. Take whatever opportunities there are, and use them as stepping-stones."

That's what we were told. But when I got to the States, things changed. I had to choose to be *better*, because I didn't feel anything like what was demanded of me to be. Couldn't fit the slot.

"Me? Dog shit? Listen close. Not only am I not dog shit . . . watch me win this race. I'm dog shit? Yeah? Watch me win."

There was simply no slot for a kid like me in a place like Florida, so I was itching to go north, despite the fact that I had no idea just how big this country was. As a teenager who tended to run away, I had made it as far as Tampa a couple of times. But my brother had six children of his own and didn't need the aggravation of having to go fetch me back in the middle of the night when I'd run out of money.

Then a summer kitchen job in the mountains of Georgia put me within striking distance of breaking out and away before Miami could register more damage on my psyche. I worked through the vacation months, and at the end of the summer I found myself in the Atlanta bus station with thirty-nine dollars in my pocket. So I had to decide where I was going to go and what I was going to do.

I knew that Miami wasn't for me, because Miami designated me, by law and social custom, as being undeserving of human consideration. While waiting at that bus station, I decided to test the waters in Atlanta. I remember taking an excursion by streetcar, roaming around for hours with all my senses alert for resemblances to the Miami of my recent acquaintance. I covered both sides of the railroad tracks, but I saw nothing that would entice me to consider dropping anchor in Atlanta. Those two southern cities were too much the same in all matters that bore directly on my situation. There was simply no room for me to be *me*. I was still running from the nightmare of Miami, looking for signs of the dreams I had left behind in more congenial places. Dreams that were holding on to me as tightly as I was holding on to them.

I soon found my way back to the bus station's ticket window, with the inquiry, "Excuse me, please, but where's the next bus going?"

"Chattanooga," said the agent, his voice rumbling through the caged window of the booth. "And it leaves in five minutes."

"How far is Chattanooga?" I asked, and he told me so many miles.

And I said, "How much is that?"

He said, "Two dollars and five cents."

"No. Not far enough," I said.

"Well, where do you want to go?" he pressed.

"Where's the next bus going after that?" I asked him.

"The next bus is going to Birmingham."

"How much is that?"

"Two forty-five."

"No. Still not far enough. Where's the next bus going after that?"

"The next bus is going to New York."

And I said, "How much is that?"

And he said, "That's eleven dollars and thirty-five cents."

And I said, "That's far enough."

"Round trip?" he asked.

"No. One way."

Most of the people in Nassau have never been to America, but still there were the myths, the tales, the stories about the country, the most enchanting of which had their roots in a legendary place called Harlem. Always Harlem. People spoke of Harlem as if it were the whole of New York City. The Apollo Theatre, Duke Ellington, Ella Fitzgerald. Harlem was the Mecca for black people in America.

So when the ticket agent said that a certain bus would be going to New York, all of the good things I'd ever heard about Harlem translated into a place that would be positively different from Florida. Florida was oppressive and Florida was mean-spirited. New York was far, far away from Florida—in miles and in promise.

So I went to New York. When I got there, my first conversation was with a well-dressed black guy from whom I sought directions on how to get to Harlem. He pointed to some steps leading down into the ground and told me to go that way. I went down those steps heading underground—and it all began. I wasn't prepared for what I saw. Never in my life had I heard of such a thing! Trains running at breakneck speed under the ground! Loaded with people! Trains swooshing by one another in different directions! Under the ground? Of New York City? If this is the way one gets to Harlem, I thought, Harlem must be one hell of a place!

THREE

THE TIME
OF ASHES

IT WOULD BE two years before I wandered into the American Negro Theatre, and they were two indispensable years. It's the way of all ancient stories. The young man must go "down" in order to find the right path for going "up." Call it the "time of ashes." In some African tribes the young boys must cover their faces with ashes before their initiation into manhood. In certain Nordic cultures the young boys used to sit down in the ashes by the fire in the center of the lodge house until they were ready to take on their adult role. And everybody knows about Cinderella, the girl who had to tend to the cinders and do all the other lowly chores until her true identity became known.

Well, for me this time of ashes was when I learned to fight for my life, when I learned what it's like to be tested and what it's like to scramble. And New York City, in its mercilessness, went about testing me without regard of any kind. As is generally the case in the time of ashes, I learned to survive with little more craft than they teach kids in Sunday school. I began to learn about balancing the good and the bad in myself, about finding the place for all sorts of energies circulating within, and about discovering how all those attributes and energies fit into the natural order of things. Most of all, I began to learn how the entirety of my person melded into one fully acceptable human being. I realized that I wasn't some Goody Two-shoes for public consumption, who kept hidden some other identity that harbored all the dark desires and deep resentments that kept popping out anyway. On the streets I developed a little mercy regarding myself as well as others, and maybe even a little wisdom.

For weeks in New York I rode those subways with a sense of wonder. I gorged myself on hotdogs and malted milkshakes. I slept on rooftops, worked in kitchens, and was close enough to at least one race riot to find myself shot in the leg and playing dead in order to avoid worse.

There were many, many close scrapes, but I was young and resilient. Often it seemed that something I could neither touch nor see—some mysterious force—had just walked me through a difficult patch or had covered my back at a crucial point. Was that something a spiritual presence? An intuitive sense? Wishful thinking?

Whatever it was, I had little time to linger over such thoughts, struggling as I was at the age of sixteen with much more immediate issues of survival.

Over a long holiday weekend I took a train to the Catskills to work as dishwasher at a famous resort. I was in an all-black group of temporary workers "imported" from New York City to beef up the hotel's manpower. In our group was a chap named Jojo Sutton. I knew that Jojo was going to be trouble the first time I saw his eyes focus on me. For no apparent reason, there were vibrations negative enough to crinkle paper. Jojo was dark of skin, with chiseled features and haunting eyes.

My first reading was "He bears watching." Looking back, it should have been "Avoid at all costs." That would have been impossible, of course, since we were obligated to work at each other's side, scraping and feeding dirty dishes into one end of a giant machine, then retrieving and stacking them by size and shape at the other end. Jojo was good on both ends, and I was past apprenticeship; so one would think we would have worked smoothly together, skill for skill. But Jojo was simply a mean and dangerous guy. To him the territory around the machine was *his* turf. *His* was the power of consequence there. I was a serf at the disposal of the emperor. Out of a sense of self-preservation, I bowed to his hallucinations with respect. I knew the long weekend would soon be over. I needed to simply hang in for the four days and get the paycheck. I concluded that Jojo, the machine, and the turf surrounding it, in combination, were all "live withable" for as long as I would have to be there.

In a small black community not far from the resort was a hoochy-cooch bar with food, music, a dance floor, and an enticing percentage of unescorted women waiting for a group of male kitchen workers to roll by about four o'clock in the afternoon in search of R&R. This mix was explosive enough without adding Jojo and his problems.

At the bottom of Jojo's list of issues was the fact that he wasn't much of a dancer. I wasn't much better, but I *was* better. And how was I to know that the girl *he* liked to dance with preferred dancing with *me?*

That afternoon, after some time on the dance floor, Jojo asked me to take a walk with him. While my mind was on full alert as we walked along a deserted path in the nearby woods, instinct was screaming at me, "Be careful!" For a while Jojo made conversation about normal guy stuff. Then he segued into profiling the kind of people he didn't like. Soon enough I started recognizing myself in his narrative. As he continued talking, I was jolted by the Jekyll and Hyde transformation I saw coming over him. As the verbal attack grew more heated and more direct, I got to wondering how best to protect myself if push came to shove. Jojo never broke his stride. His right hand simply disappeared into his right back pocket and reappeared holding a switchblade knife. The button was pushed, the blade was released, and the sweeping motion of his right hand stopped with the blade pointed inches from my chest.

I hadn't been expecting anything good, but I sure as hell wasn't expecting *that!* The element of surprise paid off. I was scared, and Jojo noticed. The knife moved up slowly toward my face. I flinched. In silence he savored my fear. He touched the blade to my cheek. He lowered it to my neck, where it rested on my jugular. He was like a maestro, slowly moving the knife to orchestrate my degree of terror.

"I oughta kill your ass right here," he said. "Who the fuck's gonna know?"

He fell silent again, his eyes still boring into me. Then he said, "You don't think I'll kill your ass, huh?"

I didn't say a word.

"Go ahead, start some shit so I can show you," he challenged.

He stepped back to give himself room in case I was dumb enough to make a move. I waited. He waited. Seconds passed. Then he abruptly turned and walked away. Thirty or so feet along, he turned back to me and said, "You watch yourself around me. You hear? You got that?"

"Yeah, I got it," I said.

As we parted ways, I had the feeling that Jojo would always try to win by intimidation.

Years later, in psychoanalysis, I would relive that moment, wondering how far I might have gone in self-defense if we had really gotten down to blows, analyzing too the range of insecurities that might have led a character like Jojo to go through life that way.

But I had another opponent about to land on my ass—one whose brute force could bear no analysis. I was about to face my first New York winter, and I simply had no idea. Coming from a tropical island, as I did, I couldn't comprehend what was about to happen as the skies began to brood in November and then let loose with the white stuff starting around Christmastime. This was not an adversary I could simply stare down while trying to stay cool. This was a months-long, relentless test of endurance. I didn't have so much as a pair of gloves. No scarf, no boots, no heavy coat—and without them I was no match for Mother Nature, not when she turned into a bitch and gave us that cold shoulder, that bony old shoulder that could literally freeze a guy's ass off—as well as his nose, his ears, and his fingers.

That winter worked me over so bad I chose the Army as a refuge. I had to lie about my age to get in, since I was just nearing seventeen, but the service did at least get me off the rooftops, and it gave me three meals a day and a warm place to sleep. But I had no more tolerance for military discipline than I did for southern Jim Crow. Which is why, in 1944, I was in custody of the U.S. Army military police, charged with assaulting a senior officer. Which is why I was thrown into the psycho ward of Mason General Hospital on Long Island, New York, and ordered to undergo psychiatric evaluation by a team of head-shrinkers to determine whether or not electroshock treatments should be administered to my brain.

From all indications, according to information supplied to the shrinks by the MPs, something had gone wrong in my head. Prominent in the Army's version was the assumption that the offending act was premeditated. They saw it as designed to appear lightning quick and seemingly impulsive but suspected that it was, in fact, a painstakingly calculated intent to do bodily harm.

In any case, there I was. Looking smack into the face of a court-martial that could effectively lock me away for twenty-five years if, in the end, I was declared to have been of sound mind when I threw a massive wooden chair at that senior officer's head.

When the raw truth surfaced, it was revealed that the Army was right in their assumption. The act *was* premeditated. Yes. *And* calculatedly designed. Yes. But *not* to do harm. My scenario called for the chair to miss that officer by inches. And in fact it did. It went crashing through the huge bay window that stretched from wall to wall behind his desk, exactly as I had planned. My overall purpose was aimed at something other than that officer's head. An excuse was my immediate objective. My actions were a shameful attempt to establish an excuse that would allow me to eventually walk away from obligations I had freely and solemnly assumed.

Simply put, I wanted to get the hell out of the Army. Nothing more lofty, nothing less worthy. But within a few days' time, I could see that throwing that chair was shaping up to have been a very bad call, a mistake I would come to wish I had never, ever made. On the drawing board of my mind, it had been laid out as the first in a series of events that would deliver me from the mess I had gotten into. The Army wasn't what I had expected—we were ill at ease with each other, didn't like each other one bit—so ... I opted to move on. Hence the "premeditated," "painstakingly designed" plan was hatched in my head, pretty much as charged. What I devised was a new approach to an old procedure for bucking out of the Army by pretending to be nuts. According to Army tradition, crazy folks had to be separated from the herd and ultimately sent away—in the best interest of the herd.

The dramatic hurling of the chair was the act chosen to initiate that process. Which it did. But another key ingredient lay at the heart of this mistake. It had a hand in the sculpting, shaping, molding, timing, editing of everything that added up to the total event, including the selection of chair-throwing as an opener. That key ingredient was inside of me. A weakness. A flaw that resided deep within. And on the afternoon the chair flew, my behavior, to my sorrow, spoke directly to the absence of character. To the presence of weakness. To the flaw that sometimes operated independent of my better judgment.

I had access to alternative pathways out of the Army. Why did I choose the approach that was a huge mistake? Was it more macho? Yes. Was it more exciting? Yes. Was it more dangerous? Yes. But most of all, it was far more irresistible to demons inside me whose existence I hadn't yet become aware of. Oh, I suspected even then that my choice was lacking in character. But I went for it anyway. And I didn't just suspect, I knew *for sure*, that my choice was of dubious value as a tactical advantage. But I went for it anyway. Reaching, it seemed, to grab hold of an intangible too complicated for the understanding of my teen years.

The alternate pathway out of the Army promised none of the charismatic power of my favored option. In no way was it a testosterone-kicker. It was the truth, and it was therefore dull. It was plain. It wasn't seductive. It didn't boogie. No euphoric highs or valley lows. No wooden chairs. No smashed bay windows. As so often happens, the absence of room for kicking the dog and disturbing the peace caused dogs to be kicked and the peace to be broken.

What transpired between the Army and me over the torturous months that followed was fascinating, bittersweet, and somewhat scary. Many of the go-rounds between the head psychiatrist and me had a hold-your-breath, cat-and-mouse quality to them. He and I each took as much as we gave. He was white, looked to be about mid-thirties, had serious eyes and an easy smile. He got me to focus on a me inside of me that no one knew, including me. In turn I taught him stuff he hadn't known, including things he'll never forget. From him I learned that on some occasions it's possible to see more than meets the eye. In some small yet meaningful way we were teachers to each other.

BY THE TIME I was eighteen years old, I was back on the street in New York, struggling once again to survive on a dishwasher's pay.

If I could have pulled together the scratch, I would have headed back to Nassau—that's how big and fierce the prospect of another winter loomed over me. I even wrote directly to President Roosevelt for a loan, hitting him up for the hundred dollars I figured it would take. If I had succeeded in that effort, I probably would have spent my life at some low-level job

taking care of tourists, spending Sundays sitting on a rock outside Nassau town trying to catch me a big fish. So even in my
lack of luck, once again I was very lucky.

One day shortly after my discharge, as I was scanning the
want-ads for dishwasher openings, an article on the theatrical
page of the *Amsterdam News*, a New York paper, caught my
attention. I was between jobs and my pockets were nearly
empty—so empty, in fact, that if no dishwashing position was
available, I was ready to glom on to any kind of work that a
black kid with no education might qualify for.

The page of want-ad boxes faced the theatrical page, on
which sat an article with a heading that read ACTORS
WANTED. The gist of the article was that a theater group called
the American Negro Theatre was in need of actors for its next
production. My mind got to spinning. My eyes bounced back
and forth between the want-ad page and the theatrical page.

"What the hell," I thought. "I've tried dishwashers wanted,
porters wanted, janitors wanted—why not try actors wanted?"
I figured that I could do the work. Acting didn't sound any
more difficult than washing dishes or parking cars. And the
article didn't say the job required any particular kind of training. But when I went in and was auditioned on the spot, the
man in charge quickly let me know—and in no uncertain
terms—that I was misguided in my assumptions. I had no
training in acting. I could barely read! And to top it off, I had a
thick, singsong Bahamian accent.

He snatched the script from my hands, spun me around,
grabbed me by the scruff of my neck and the back of my pants,

and marched me on my tippytoes toward the door. He was seething. "You just get out of here and stop wasting people's time. Go get a job you can handle," he barked. And just as he threw me out, he ended with, "Get yourself a job as a dishwasher or something."

I have to tell you that his comments stung worse than any wasp on any sapodilla tree back in my childhood. His assessment was like a death sentence for my soul. I had never mentioned to him that I was a dishwasher. How did he know? If he *didn't* know, what was it about me that implied to this stranger that dishwashing would accurately sum up my whole life's worth?

Whatever it was, I knew I had to change it, or life was going to be mighty grim. There's something inside me—pride, ego, sense of self—that hates to fail at anything. I could never accept such a verdict of failure before I'd even begun my life! So I set out on a course of self-improvement. I worked nights, and on my evening meal-breaks I sat in a quiet area of the restaurant where I was employed, near the entrance to the kitchen, reading newspapers, trying to sound out each syllable of each unfamiliar word. An old Jewish waiter, noticing my efforts, took pity and offered to help. He became my tutor, as well as my guardian angel of the moment. Each night we sat in the same booth in that quiet area of the restaurant and he helped me learn to read.

My immediate objective was to prove that I could be an actor. Not that I had any real desire to go on the stage, mind you. Not that I had ever given acting a thought before reading that ad. I simply needed to prove to that man at the American

Negro Theatre that Sidney Poitier had a hell of a lot more to him than washing dishes.

And it worked. The second time around they let me in. But it was still no slam dunk. In fact, I made the cut only because there were so few guys and they needed some male bodies to fill the new acting class. But soon after that first hurdle went down, another went up: because of my lack of education and experience, after a couple of months I was flunking out. And once again I felt that vulnerability, as if I'd fallen overboard into deep water. If I lost my chance at the theater, where would I be? One more black kid who could barely read washing dishes on the island of Manhattan. So I worked out a deal. I became their janitor, and they let me continue to study.

Things began to improve, and maybe even I began to improve—as an actor, that is. But when it was time to cast the first big production, in walked this new guy, another kid from the Caribbean with whom the director had worked before. After all my studies, busting my ass trying to learn to act (not to mention busting my ass sweeping the walk and stoking the furnace), she was going to cast *him* in the lead. Well, I had to admit he was a pretty good-looking kid, and he had a nice voice. He could even sing a little.

I tried to find some consolation in the fact that they made me the understudy, but little did I know. On the night of the first major run-through, the one night a significant casting director was coming to watch the show, the other Caribbean kid they'd cast for the lead—a kid named Harry Belafonte—couldn't make it. I had to go on for him, and son of a gun, the casting director liked what I did and called me.

"I'm preparing a version of *Lysistrata* for Broadway. Would you be available?"

Are you kidding?

Next thing I knew I was staring out into a sea of white faces from a Broadway stage, scared shitless as I fumbled for my lines as Polydorus.

The word *bad* cannot begin to accommodate my wretchedness. I mean, I was BAD. The stage fright had me so tightly in its grip that I was giving the wrong cues and jumbling the lines, and within a few moments the audience was rolling in the aisles.

The moment the curtain came down it was time for this Caribbean kid to run for cover. My career was over before it had begun, and the void was opening up once again to receive me. I didn't even go to the cast party, which meant that I wasn't around when the first reviews appeared.

The critics trashed the show. I mean, they *hated* it. But they liked me. I was so god-awful they thought I was good. They said they admired my "fresh, comedic gift."

If you saw this scenario in an old black-and-white movie on TV, would you believe it? I saw it in real life, and I certainly didn't. In my world, effort and reward were expected to settle into a natural balance. By any reasonable measure, I knew that I'd fallen short that evening. That was *my* critical assessment. That assessment, taken at its worth, created a big fat contradiction inside me. Maybe I just wasn't up to this acting thing.

Maybe the man at the little theater in Harlem was right. Maybe I *should* "go out and get a job I could handle."

I couldn't shake the sense that failure was lurking somewhere in the wings, waiting to pick my bones if my doubts should become reality. Still, in the face of all that, I had to stay in charge of my life no matter how it all played out. Regardless of whatever (or whoever) else might have been looking out for me, I needed to know, first and foremost, that *I* was looking out for *myself*. Even when the dread of being shot down by failure twisted my insides into knots.

Did I misjudge this new culture? Should all the glitter that now seemed only inches beyond my reach have been taken with a grain of salt? Maybe natural balances weren't that easily found amid so much concrete and steel. Amid so many machines pushing automobiles, lifting elevators, pulling trains. Or maybe, at the very bottom, I wasn't yet ready to accept that environment compromises values far more than values do their number on environment.

The play ran only four days. But to my surprise, my "triumph" in *Lysistrata* led immediately to another acting job as an understudy in a road show of *Anna Lucasta*, a job that lasted intermittently for several weeks. Then, after a long, lean, and frustrating period, during which off-Broadway roles happened by just often enough to keep my meager skills alive, I found out quite by accident that 20th Century–Fox was casting for a movie called *No Way Out*, the film that would be the first that Reggie and Evelyn Poitier would ever see.

My fingers touched the glitter with that first movie, and it was a mighty reach, I tell you. I knew full well how far I had come from those days in Nassau when I dreamed of being a "cowboy" in Hollywood.

While I was completing that Fox picture in L.A., the film's director, Joseph Mankiewicz, told me that when I got back to New York I should look up a producer named Zoltan Korda. I did, entering his office just as he was walking out. "No time to talk," he said. "Can you come to London?"

Next thing I knew I was on the Pan Am *Clipper* in a first-class compartment heading east across the Atlantic, bound for London and eventually South Africa, to play the part of the young priest in *Cry, the Beloved Country.*

It was heady stuff, and I couldn't escape the feeling that, not only was I one lucky youngster, but something more had to be at play here. I had grown up in a culture where unseen forces lurked just out of view, where people looked to "the mysteries" to explain both good fortune and bad. As I tried to absorb the changes in my new life, I butted up against the knowledge that this many accidents and lucky breaks just didn't happen in the movie business, or anywhere else. They didn't even happen in the movies themselves! I knew that things could be taken away just as easily as they now seemed to come. I rested uneasily on those black-and-white and scary uncertainties.

After returning from London I at last went back to the Bahamas and came very much back down to earth. I saw my mother and my father for the first time in eight years. I had gone away a troubled boy of fifteen, and here I was, a man of twenty-three whom they could hardly recognize. It was a powerful moment when I returned to our little house in Nassau and saw them sitting together, alone, on a Saturday night. It was a moment of miraculous joy, but also a time of wrenching guilt for me, because during those eight years I had remained entirely silent.

It's an unwritten law in the Bahamas that when people who go to America to live write home, they put a little something in the envelope. I had been unable to contribute to my family for so long that the habit of silence had simply overtaken me. Or at least that's how I had justified it to myself. I had to wait until I was in good shape, I had told myself. Still, I knew that *Reggie* was more of a man than to let eight years pass without a word.

I made amends, but my guilt wasn't canceled. My parents forgave me—they would have forgiven me anything—and I left with them almost all of the three thousand dollars I had made in my nascent career in the movies. But I knew that, forced to take my measure at that moment, even they would have found me wanting.

So going back to New York was a valuable exercise in humility. After that initial burst of success—a couple of films and a couple of major theatrical productions—I was back in Harlem washing dishes. Perhaps I had a gift from Cat Island buried deep within me, because despite the setback, I still had faith in myself and faith in the future—enough of each to marry a beautiful young girl named Juanita and try to get on with my life. Then a buddy of mine had the bright idea of opening a rib place. We scraped together the money and opened a little joint, Ribs in the Ruff (at 127th Street and 7th Avenue), with seating for all of thirteen people.

My wife was trying her hand at modeling, though that led by way of necessity to a job as a seamstress at a clothing factory. This life was tough, but we were up for it. Having lived with my mother and my father, having watched how they dealt with other people and with each other, I felt prepared for pretty much anything.

Soon our first child was born, little Beverly, and then another was on her way, and I didn't have any money. Our little barbecue place was a hole in the wall. Eighty cents for a meal, including side dishes. My partner and I did everything. We cooked the ribs, we made the potato salad, we made the coleslaw, we scrubbed out the place when we closed in the morning. Times were so tough that I used to take milk from the restaurant home for my kid.

One day when my wife was pregnant with Pam, I was working in the rib joint. I was tapped out and feeling worried. That day, with nothing encouraging in sight, out of the blue a big agent named Marty Baum called me and said, "Would you come down? I have something I want to talk to you about."

He wasn't *my* agent, of course. He was just helping out on a casting assignment. His office was on 5th Avenue, between 58th and 57th Streets.

He said, "Go over to the Savoy Plaza Hotel, suite such and such. There's a gentleman who wants to see you about a part."

I went over. Two guys were there, the producer and the director. We had a very brief talk, they looked me over a bit, and one of them said, "We'd like you to read for us."

I said, "Certainly."

They gave me a script, asked me to turn to a particular page, and gave me a few moments to look over the scene. When I thought I was ready, I said, "Okay." They had me read the scene with the producer while the director watched.

I felt good about the reading, though they didn't say much about it. They asked me things about my life and what I had done in the business, and I told them. They gave me a script to take with me and said they would talk to Marty Baum. They thanked me for coming as I left.

I went back and said to Marty Baum, "They gave me a script." He said, "Well, read it. Call me tomorrow, and we'll work out something."

I went straight home—127th Street, near Amsterdam Avenue—and I read the script. I didn't like it. The part they wanted me for was a man who was a janitor for a gambling casino in Phenix City, Alabama. He was a very nice man, but there had been some kind of murder at the casino, and it was thought that this janitor might have some information that could incriminate whoever was responsible. He received threats and warnings to keep his mouth shut, so he didn't do anything, didn't say anything. Then, to augment the threat, the bad guys killed his young daughter, throwing her body on his lawn. He was enraged. He was tormented. Still, he remained passive. He didn't do shit. He left it to other people to fight his battles.

So the next day I went back to Marty Baum's office.

"What do you think of the script?" he asked.

"Well, I have to tell you, I'm not going to play it," I said.

Disbelief etched his face. "You're not gonna play it?"

"No," I said. "I *can't* play it."

"What do you mean you can't play it?" he asked, irritated.

"I cannot play it," I repeated.

"It's not a derogatory part," he pointed out.

"No, it's not."

"What happens to this guy isn't a racial thing," he said.

"Not necessarily," I agreed. "It could happen to any guy in that particular set of circumstances."

"So what is it?" he said. "I mean, is it . . . ?" He paused, apparently trying to make sense of my response. "They don't call you names, they don't—" He went on to say they're not doing this to you, they're not doing that to you.

I said, "Yeah, that's all true."

"Then what *is* it?" he urged.

"I can't tell you," I said, "but there's something about it. I just don't want to go into it."

So he said to me, "Well, listen, that's the way it goes. But I still don't understand."

I thanked him and left. Then I went over to 57th Street and Broadway, one flight up, to a place called Household Finance Company, and I borrowed seventy-five dollars on the furniture in our apartment, because I needed the money. The birth of our second daughter was fairly near, and I knew that Beth Israel Hospital was going to cost me seventy-five bucks, so I had to line up the money.

Six months later I got a call. "Hello. Sidney Poitier?"

"Yes," I answered.

"This is Marty Baum."

"Oh, yes, how are you, sir?" I said.

"Fine. How are you? What are you doing?" he asked.

I said, "I'm still in the restaurant, working."

He said, "You haven't had any jobs as an actor?"

"No, I haven't," I said.

He said, "Come down. I want to talk to you."

So I went down to the Baum and Newborn offices, across from the Plaza. They had two or three other agents, and three or four secretaries. I went into Marty Baum's private office, and he sat me down.

"I don't have a job for you," he said, "but I asked you to come down because I wanted to say something to you." He stared at me in silence for a moment before continuing. "You know, I've never met anybody like you. That part was a pretty good part. It had no racial overtones to it, and you turned it down. You haven't done anything since, and it would have been—well, it was paying 750 dollars a week. It would have been a nice piece of change."

He once again asked me to explain why I hadn't taken the part, but all I could say was, "Well, you know, it's the way I am."

He said, "Well, I'll tell you what. I don't know what's going on with you, but anybody as crazy as you, I want to handle him."

I said, "Okay." And that's how I landed with a big agent, and that's when my career got on solid footing.

Now, I couldn't tell him at the time, and maybe it'll sound a little sanctimonious even now, after all these years, but I rejected that part because, in my view, the character simply didn't measure up. He didn't fight for what mattered to him most. He didn't behave with dignity.

My father, Reggie, was a certain kind of man, and he was a certain kind of dad. He was a poor man, for certain. He was a hard-working man, for sure. The only thing he knew how to do was tomato farming, but the soil in Nassau wasn't good, and it was a tourist economy, and there was simply no room for him to plant. By this time he was fifty or fifty-five, and he was suffering severely from rheumatoid arthritis, among other things. He had worked in a bicycle shop in Nassau, but after some years he'd lost the job. The only way he could make a living now was to have my brother in Miami send him boxes of very cheap cigars. My father would then spend the day walking around town, going from one bar to another, selling the cigars. One to this person, two to another. That's how poor he was. But he did what he had to do. And I wasn't going to play any part that might dishonor his values.

My mom, too, always measured up. She would go scouring the neighborhood and into the nearby woods, picking up rocks and stones—sometimes as much as twenty-pound stones or thirty-pound stones, even fifty-pound stones. When she had gathered upwards of two thousand pounds into a mound in the yard in front of our house, she would sit under an almond tree with a hammer in her hand and a big wide straw hat on her head, and from morning to night she would hammer those stones into pebbles and those pebbles into gravel.

It would take her weeks to break a pile of stones that reached close to ceiling height in a pyramid fashion. That's a hell of a lot of stones to break. And she didn't work at it just for a few weeks; the weeks would sometimes run into months. When she had an impressive enough pyramid of crushed stones—mind you, other poor women were doing the same thing—a man would come by with his truck and his workers, and he would bargain with her for her pyramid of crushed stones, and he would pay her whatever she was able to negotiate—on average, ten shillings, twelve shillings, a pound and a half. Fifteen shillings would have been the equivalent of about six dollars. The man would pay her the six dollars, or whatever it was, and his workmen would shovel all the gravel into his truck, and they would go.

Then, after some respite of a week or so, she would start gathering stones all over again.

But what Reggie and Evelyn did for a living in no way articulated who they were as people. There was this whole race/class thing in the Bahamas, and among blacks the class thing was prevalent and vigorously administered. If you were really poor, you were without leverage and powerless, and that was the majority of the people. Also, there was a class of blacks who felt they were above you. They mimicked the colonial value system and saw themselves at the top of the black community. It was their hierarchical sort of thing. Well, my dad was so poor that he was dismissed by the black social structure, dismissed by *every* social structure. Dismissed by everyone, pretty much, except his friends. He had lots of friends.

Now trust me, the man never complained. These are *my* complaints, not *his*. No complaints. He was there, life was as it was—that's how he looked at it. He knew what kind of a person he was.

He knew what kind of a family he had. He knew what kind of a woman he was married to. He had no money; he had to squeeze a living out of the most unusual activities, but everything he undertook was honorable, because that was who he was.

And Evelyn, of course, I never heard her complain—never, not once—though she *would* get a little pissed at me when I grumbled about the kind of clothes I had. I was simply too young to understand our situation, but she may have translated my complaints into an implication of failure on her part or Dad's. In any case, she had answers for that, you know? And the answers were damn good ones, and they had no self-pity in them, and they had no self-incrimination in them. She would say the kinds of things that proud and honorable poor mothers have always said—things like, "As long as the clothes you have are clean, they're fine."

But when I got to New York, and when I got to Hollywood, for whatever reason or by whatever stroke of luck, I was given the tremendous opportunity of doing work that could reflect who I was. And who I was had everything to do with Reggie and Evelyn and each cigar sold and each rock broken. That's how I've always looked at it: that my work is who I am. I decided way back at the beginning, back when I was still washing dishes in a barbecue joint in Harlem, that the work I did would never bring dishonor to my father's name.

I do what I do for me and for my wife and children, of course. And I do it out of a certain professional ego-drive and ambition like anyone else. But everything I do, I also do for Reggie and for Evelyn.

FOUR

LIFE IN BLACK AND WHITE

MY HAPHAZARD political education got underway in 1943. The school in which that education occurred was that district north of Central Park known as Harlem, New York.

Now, the school of hard knocks provided no classes in political science, but long before I arrived, Harlem residents knew full well that politics was a deck stacked against them—an invisible force of exclusion expertly woven into the fabric of everyday life. In the school of hard knocks, politics was a name for the way white folks arranged things to their own advantage.

Harlem residents had figured a good many things out. (1) They knew that for practical, economic reasons, there never was a time when downtown politics didn't embrace Harlem as a cheap and handy labor pool. (2) In cultural terms, they knew of downtown politics' insistence on a requisite distance being kept once the day's work was done. (3) They knew that in matters of race, downtown politics had set in place rules and ways to enforce those rules, to ensure that all residents from Harlem were respectful of the "civilized traditions" that had been erected between themselves and the larger community over the preceding two hundred years. (4) They also knew that when need required, downtown politics would bombard Harlem with promises Harlem's residents knew, from experience, would never materialize.

The Harlem that I knew for fourteen years was an amazing place—a fabled destination well known in African-American communities throughout the country. Its dazzling power drew visitors of many races from many places to experience by taste, by smell, by touch its bewitching energies, its mysterious vibrations, and its signature rhythms, each of which was said to be in the very air a visitor breathed. And all of Harlem's visitors were encouraged to believe that each breath they took would also contain spiritual blessings that came flowing out of the soul of its loving people through the gateways of their hearts.

Harlem's attractions beckoned with a wink and a smile. Jazz at Minton's. Vaudeville at the Apollo. Floor shows at Smalls' Paradise. Comedians and torch singers at the Baby Grand. Jitterbuggers at the Savoy and the Renaissance Casino. Soul food at Jennylou's. Elegant late-night dining at Wells. The Palm. Frank's. Sugar Ray Robinson's. The Shalamar. Joe's

Barbecue. And after midnight, when the legitimate bars closed, the speakeasies would open. There was gambling at the Rhythm Club twenty-four hours a day. There were pleasure houses offering high-quality interludes at prices that guaranteed satisfaction. And then there was the Theresa Hotel—a symbol of community pride and joy—where visitors of big-time status would hold court. Dignitaries from the Caribbean, Africa, South America, and elsewhere. Showbiz heavyweights like the Duke of Ellington, the Count of Basie. Jimmie Lunceford. Louis Jordan. Billy Eckstine. Dinah Washington. Sarah Vaughan. Ruth Brown. And countless others. But the most memorable characters of all appeared suddenly out of another life, and just as suddenly disappeared again.

Baron Smith, for example, was a tall, large-framed, brown-skinned man of some three hundred or more pounds who never failed to cut a most imposing figure when he entered or exited the lobby of the Theresa Hotel. Perhaps he would be impeccably done up in a white doeskin double-breasted suit, with a boutonniere in his lapel, a Panama hat sitting slightly forward on his head, two-toned black-and-white shoes on his feet, and an emerald-and-diamond ring on his left-hand pinkie finger—an ensemble that, taken together, served as perfect background for an elegant, black, custom-made shirt and the Savile Row necktie that completed the picture. Next day, perhaps an off-white linen suit, with equally arresting accessories. The following day, an entirely new look yet again.

Each summer, this man of substance would return to be eagerly received by the hotel's management and staff, as well as other establishments in Harlem, including certain ladies of the evening who had been graced by his presence and his wallet on previous visits.

But Baron Smith's image and presence were a tailor-made fabrication. A performance mounted for a week's run on the stage of Harlem's hot spots, with annual revivals scheduled for as many summers as the traffic would bear.

The real life of the real Baron Smith was set in Nassau, Bahamas. There he was a barkeeper who sold rum to the locals. His barroom was of modest size, and so were his sales. His profit margin had to ignore other obligations in order to cover his seven-day pilgrimage to Harlem each summer. But dream-chasers and sacrifices are never strangers for long. My father used to make daily stops at Baron Smith's barroom to sell cigars to the Baron's customers. Life in Nassau was pretty routine and uneventful for Mr. Smith. It didn't boogie. He yearned for a wild-side excitement, but all he could manage was a week of living on the edge in the ideal manner, in the perfect setting, in the flawless background of his dreams. Harlem, New York.

I knew Mr. Smith quite well. When I was twelve or thereabouts, I used to sneak into the local movie house through a small ventilation window at the rear of the theater, behind the screen. The window was too high for me to reach from the outside, so an accomplice was necessary. I would stand on the shoulders of my friend Yorick, and once safely through the window, I would reach back, grab Yorick's wrists, and haul him up and in. We then would slither under a thick curtain hanging over an entranceway that separated the backstage area from the theater itself, slither on under the first few rows of seats, and pop up innocently in the fourth or fifth row. There we would sit, doing our best to look like regular, paying customers. After roughly a dozen or so successes, one day we popped up, took our seats, and—guess what? Standing over us was Mr. Baron Smith. He was the manager of the movie house in those earlier days.

He grabbed us by the back of our collars, lifted us to our feet, and marched us to his office as pictures of reform school flashed through our heads. We knew that if he called the cops, an example would be made of us as a warning to all young males of similar age and reckless persuasion. That would mean six years in the slammer for each of us.

He sat us down in the privacy of his office. "I know your father," he said to me. "What do you think he would say if he knew what you've been doing?"

Yorick and I knew that the question wasn't meant to be answered, so we sat quietly. The lecture was short, but it found its mark.

"Now, get out of here," he said, after letting us stew a few minutes. "If you try something like this again, you'll regret it the rest of your lives. What you did is as bad as stealing. You don't want to grow up to be thieves, do you? Thieves wind up in jail; remember that. Honesty really is the best policy."

We weren't going to *wind up* as thieves. We *were* thieves already. But we weren't going to compound our problems by being honest enough to divulge *that* information. Mr. Smith escorted us out to the street and let us fly away. Free as birds.

Sixty years have passed since Mr. Smith let Yorick and me walk, but the generosity he displayed was a great lesson for me. Likewise, I learned much from Harlem's generosity in welcoming Baron Smith with his image as a man of importance, wealth, generosity, and presence (all fashioned with *clothing and pretense*) and its generosity in keeping such dreams alive for Baron Smith and dreamers like him from all over the world.

For Baron Smith the dreamer, Harlem was a stage-setting reflecting mere images of reality; but the fact is we the people of Harlem were real. Consequently, Harlem nourished another kind of dreamer to speak to our concerns. As a young man I began to ask myself, Who is speaking for me, and who is speaking to me? And as the saying goes, "When the student is ready, the teacher appears."

From the pages of newspapers, from the radio, from newsreels in the movie houses, and from poems and sermons, teachers— men of vision and courage from all walks of life—began to appear. One by one they spoke to me, and they spoke *for* me. Paul Robeson, Dr. Ralph Bunche, A. Philip Randolph, Adam Clayton Powell, Jr., Roy Wilkins, Mary McCloud Bethune, Walter White, Whitney Young, Langston Hughes. And others. And in the course of time the voices of newfound friends from my generation, including William Garfield Greaves, Harry Belafonte, Leon Bibb, Philip and Doris Rose, William Branch, William Marshall, Julian Mayfield, and others, would be added. Like me, they were young. Unlike me, they were not political greenhorns. These intelligent young people—Harry Belafonte, Leon Bibb, and Philip and Doris Rose most especially—would become and remain invaluable contributors to my political education. By their example and my own intense effort at reading the newspapers, I picked up useful bits of basic information every day.

In 1945, at eighteen years of age and fresh out of the Army, I was unaware, for instance, what it meant to be a "Democrat," a "Republican," a "progressive," a "socialist," a "communist," an "anarchist," a "northern liberal," a "southern conservative." Nor had I a clue as to how people who earned those labels differed from one another. It took some time before I came to understand who among the spokespeople for these various positions were genuine allies of those who spoke for the men and women of Harlem, and for the youngsters of my generation. But by the age of twenty-one, I had grown familiar with the landscape and had acquired a general understanding of what was driving each major player philosophically.

My teachers came in a wide variety of forms and in a great variety of locales. Louise, for example, lived in Brooklyn, and the trip from the American Negro Theatre on 127th Street in Harlem to her doorstep was a long ride. I offered to see her home one night after a late rehearsal at the theater, and I would wind up making that trip time after time.

Saintly, volatile, edgy, raucous, bitchy, introspective, sensuous, a talented and daring taker of risks—that was Louise. In acting classes she was a riveting, hypnotic presence. As a nineteen-year-old black girl, she was often mistaken for Arabic, or Asian, or Native American. She was, in fact, a mixed-race person of African-American and white descent, but she claimed only her African-American heritage.

Talking with her was a pleasure, mainly because I wasn't interested as much in getting into her pants as getting into her mind. She seemed to know a little bit about everything, and I knew she could help me fill in the blanks in my own general knowledge. Her words touched familiar chords I had often heard inside myself, her voice lodging complaints we both held against the state.

Her language, too, inspired me. For instance, the phrases "rhetorical bullshit" and "disingenuous motherfucker." "Bullshit" and "motherfucker" I had heard before, of course, but what kind of bullshit gets to be "rhetorical," and what need a motherfucker do to be considered a "disingenuous motherfucker"? "Bourgeoisie Negroes" was another. We got locked in a conversation once, I remember, about who she was and who I was, as individuals, in America. "How we see our-selves, how we see each other," she said, "should be deter-mined by us and not by people who generally don't like us; people who pass laws certifying us as less than human. Too many of us see each other as 'they' see us," she continued. "Time for that shit to stop. We're going to have to decide for ourselves what we are and what we're not. Create our own image of ourselves. And nurture it and feed it till it can stand on its own."

She looked through the plate-glass window of a coffee shop at snow falling on the Brooklyn street near where she lived. "I'll tell you one thing," she added. "If I have anything to say about it, by the time my grandchildren get here, this hypocrisy democracy is gonna do some changing."

More than a few times I asked myself if she was just regur-
gitating stuff she had heard at home from a father who was up
on such things, or a mother who was book-smart, or some
school she had attended. But then I would feel the passion
behind her words and know that she spoke from conviction.

"Things that get sandwiched in between 'differing opin-
ions,' 'opposite positions,' 'opposing views'—these are issues,"
she explained. "All things social, political, religious, financial,
personal or impersonal, objective or subjective, over which
debates are held, fights are triggered, and wars are fought—
these are issues."

Louise taught me much, not the least of which was to appre-
ciate how much a greater command of the language can enrich
one's life.

But our time was short. I soon was off to Broadway, then on
the road for several years with the play *Anna Lucasta*, then off
to Hollywood for three decades. I lost track of Louise. All my
attempts to reconnect proved fruitless. If she survived, and if
she had children, it's not farfetched to imagine them as having
been among those young African-Americans of the sixties
who sat in at southern lunch counters. Who braved "Bull"
Connor's dogs. Who put themselves on the line to end segre-
gation. Who worked at taking the "hypocrisy out of democracy," as she was so fond of saying. If Louise is still here, she
knows that the times have changed. If she's not, then I'm here
to witness for us both that the times indeed have changed.

WHEN I WAS COMFORTABLE on Cat Island, I was pulled out and placed in Nassau. When I had gotten some comfort in Nassau, which took some adjusting to, I was pulled out and placed in a hostile environment called Florida. Again and again I found myself having to leave behind the comfort gained and move on. After a time it became a ritual.

For a while it was New York, and then it was California. It was the various plays and movies and venues of the acting profession. It was the social friends that I would meet and develop at all the levels of my life. Most of these friends were eventually left behind. The moving-on lifestyle I had adopted (though not initially by choice) placed all my friendships in perpetual jeopardy. I became a loner, a separate traveler.

I always saw things differently than other people. I heard things differently. I viewed the future differently. Most times I asked of myself much more than I was able to give. I came close to self-destruction on any number of occasions. I unquestionably had to be lucky, since my struggle for survival was no more than a patchwork of trial-and-error. And I've got to tell you, there was a satisfaction, a pleasure—no, a *thrill*—in whatever successes happened as a result of dancing close to the flame and beating the odds. In just being lucky.

Telling myself I would probably lose took the edge off being afraid to lose. "Prepare for the worst; hope for the best." I did that a lot. That was the credo that enabled me to get from crisis to crisis.

Survival pressed me into being more of a serious fellow than I would have liked. But not to the complete exclusion of *some* delight and *some* joy. Only in the Bahamas, however, was delight taken fully, without reservation.

A survival tactic that worked well for me was one I had gotten from my mother: "Charm them, son," she said, "into neutral." Being charming bought me time by allowing me to at least temporarily deflect the jabs of a threatening society.

You can see, within the context of how I lived and how I was beginning to work out a relationship between myself and this complex place, that I wasn't free to indulge totally in delights. There *were* delights; there *were* indulgences. But I never lost sight of the fact that I had to cover my back, that I was always onstage.

Society had created laws to keep me at a distance, or out of sight altogether. Learning to survive in that often-hostile world was trial-and-error, step-by-step; and just as when I was learning to pick fruit from the sapodilla trees, I often got stung.

"Oh, so that's how *that* works," I would realize. So my closet is full of encounters and mistakes and tools and lessons learned truly the hard way.

After I got out of the Army and started at the American Negro Theatre, I was more of an observer than most. I was from a black culture in the Caribbean, but it was wonderful being a part of the black culture of New York. Life had another rhythm there. Boundaries were emotional and physical, but they didn't confine the spirit. There were so many places where one could find welcome and ease. Delight was plentiful. And fully taken by many, as far as I could tell from conversations overheard and behavior observed.

I was, however, also involved in white society. That's where I went to work. That's where the movie houses were, for the most part. That's where 42nd Street was. I was always going into that world. The lights of Broadway kept drawing me. On a Saturday night you got dressed and you went downtown, you know?—drawn by the busyness of it. You just walked around and—well, you got addicted to the electricity.

There was a multitude of things taken for granted by the city's longtime residents that had to be learned, practiced, rehearsed. Like depositing a nickel and dialing a public pay-phone—though at the time I learned that I didn't know one solitary person in the whole city, much less anyone who had a telephone. Learning street names and signs. Learning subway and bus routes. Learning where I was welcome and where I was not. Learning to listen harder, look deeper and further beyond that which first meets the eye. Especially since hustlers and pimps sometimes look like doctors and lawyers, no less than doctors and lawyers sometimes operate like hustlers and pimps.

The workaday heads of families—blue-collar and professional, downtown and in Harlem—had to become as readable for me as their Bahamian counterparts had in the city of Nassau. Only quicker in this American city, where time itself seemed to be a currency—the only kind I would have enough of.

By the time I had reached my early twenties, I had fought many battles, lost many wars, and lived many lives (unprepared for each of them). Life offered no auditions for the many roles I had to play. And nowhere along the roads I traveled can I recall ever hearing the word "outsider" applied to me. I had for years considered myself an old hand at the game of staying alive. But with failure walking in my shadow every minute, waiting for the misstep that could derail my whole existence, "survivor" seemed to me a more appropriate label under which my life should be filed.

Over time, however, I began to notice the frequency with which "outsider" was applied to others. The term began to resonate with me, causing me to wonder who I was really, at the center of myself. Eventually, I came to see myself in the outsider, and the outsider in me. I knew that outsider and survivor often work as partners, but they're not twins.

What was it about outsiders, I wondered, that attracted the curiosity of others? What made such personalities tick? What were the forces driving them—forces that kept them intact and in motion, moving to the beat of their own drum, no matter what? Was theirs a way of life rooted in sacrifice and challenge in defense of nobler purposes and higher values? Or was it a lifestyle of out-of-control appetites in a materialistic environment? Were outsiders simply trespassers, obliged by the nature of their lives to be constantly on the alert, known as "one of those" but never as "one of us"?

For me as a young man, the most relevant question was, How might such an outsider expect his life to unfold? What were the penalties? What beauties occurred and what scars resulted from all those times when a life-altering situation suddenly jumped in his face, blocked his path, issued a threat, or laid down a challenge? Daring him to pass through if he were foolish enough to think he had the stuff to do so. "You gotta get by me, if survival is what you're after. So suit up, Mr. Outsider. To get where you think you want to go, you have five minutes to become a flesh-and-blood person walking in shoes you've never even tried on. *But first you've got to outmaneuver me.*"

Only in my sixties did I fully absorb my outsider status and begin to settle into some kind of comfort with it. I'd been on the fringes for fifty-odd years whether I knew it or not, so at last I accepted the likelihood that I would *always* be an outsider.

I live in Beverly Hills now, but I'm still an outsider there. And Hollywood let me know my place from the beginning. Back at Columbia in the early days I was doing a picture called *All the Young Men*. Cast and crew combined were close to a hundred people, and I was the only black person on the set. I qualified hands down as the quintessential outsider. Accordingly, I felt very much as if I were representing fifteen, eighteen million people with every move I made.

One guy in particular, an electrical grip, took great delight in asking the cinematographer if he wanted to use a tiny spotlight to highlight my eyes. Whenever the cinematographer said yes, the grip would shout across the soundstage for one to be fetched by his subordinates. The N word was a nickname for that particular spotlight, and this guy used it with relish.

Years later, Arthur Ashe made reference in his book to the many times in his professional life when his response to similar situations wasn't his *natural* response, but rather the *calculated* response required of someone walking on the edge. Johnny

Johnson of *Ebony* magazine and Berry Gordy, Jr., of Motown have spoken of the same experience. Long-term outsiders know that struggling on the edge can be beneficial in ways more far-reaching than the personal reward any individual outsider might reap. Ashe, as a black man in a white sport, became an ambassador for this country. When he went to South Africa with the U.S. Tennis Association, he had to be "accommodated"; he had to be dealt with. Outsiders know that their struggle is being watched. Silently, often dangerously, they bear witness.

In the early fifties I made the rounds of every casting office in New York City, and I would walk through and stick my head in and say hello, and the secretaries and the receptionists and even the agents themselves got to know me.

It was in 1954 that a guy from the New York office of MGM called and said, "We're doing a film, and we're looking for some young actors."

I said, "How young?"

"Well, you know, it's gonna be high school."

I said, "Oh, yes, I know some guys." I automatically eliminated myself because I was about twenty-seven years old at the time.

I gave them a list of these actors, and they were in touch with them, but they called me back and asked if I would stop in for a test. Well, we did the test, and they sent it to California, and Richard Brooks, the director, was interested. Then they looked at my other pictures, whatever else I had done, and lo and behold, they offered me the part.

Now in New York City, as a black actor in the theater, there weren't but so many things coming my way. As a matter of fact, Broadway had almost nothing for a black man. Over a period of years there was *Lost in the Stars* and a play called *Deep Are the Roots. Porgy and Bess* and a few other musical presentations were in the repertoire, but with all the black actors and singers and dancers available in New York City, trying for careers in the theater, there wasn't enough work to fill a thimble, as my mother used to say. Naturally, there were those of us for whom that didn't sit right in terms of fairness.

I mean, in those days, there would be forty-odd plays on Broadway, but none having to do with *our* culture, *our* community, *our* lives. We used to petition the Actors' Equity Association, and we would try to raise the question of more employment opportunities for us, but those of us who petitioned wound up being blacklisted. I was one of the young black actors who became persona non grata, charged with being a troublemaker.

The head of the Negro Actors Guild was a man named Leigh Whipper, whom I considered to be in cahoots with the very forces that were trying to keep us out of sight and out of involvement and out of participation. One day, on 125th Street at 7th Avenue, I ran into Mr. Whipper as he came out of a little tobacco store on the northwest corner of the intersection. He spotted me, walked right up, and started chastising me about my friends, meaning my leftwing friends. Then he got personal.

Whipper felt that we blacks should be accommodating and take whatever the system was able to give. This guy was a lot older than I was, so I didn't say anything disrespectful to him; I just listened to what he said. He was blowing off his steam and getting hotter under the collar, and then he said, "Look at this, look at this." He opened his coat and there was a gun stuck in the waistband of his pants, and he said that he would use it on me and all my friends if we fucked with him. But I wasn't a fuck-wither, you know?

So I just kept my cool, and I let him blow. And when he was finished dressing me down and appeared satisfied that he had put me in my place, he walked away. But what he was telling me wasn't new. I mean, as young black actors we all knew that he was rabidly against the way we saw things.

Well, that was the background, mind you, against which I got this particular job offer from MGM.

I went out to California to do the movie *Blackboard Jungle*. I went to the wardrobe fitting, I did all the necessary preliminaries, and I met with the cast. We did the first reading and were scheduled to start work in four or five days.

Then I got a call from the front office, from one of the studio lawyers. He said, "Could you come up? I'd like to talk to you for a second."

I said, "Sure."

I went up to the front office to meet this man, a man I didn't know from Adam, and he said to me, "You know, we've been told that you know some people who are questionable characters."

"What people are you talking about?" I asked, though I knew instantly what he meant.

Then he came clean and said, "Paul Robeson. Canada Lee."

These, of course, were some of the most stand-up people in those days for things racial, and I was proud to be associated with them.

I said, "So what is it that you want from me?"

He said, "Well, we need you to sign a loyalty oath."

And I said, "What am I supposed to do by signing the oath? I must swear what?" It drove me wild that these men could see red but couldn't see black. That was galling enough. But what also appalled me was that I was being accused of being sympathetic toward, respectful of, even admiring of Paul Robeson and Canada Lee—men I *did* respect tremendously! How could I *not* admire men of such courage and integrity? Robeson had come to my house and played with my children, which filled me with pride. I got to know him well enough that he became concerned about me, urging me to be careful in my association with him.

Well, this studio lawyer—it seemed to me he didn't fully believe in what he was doing. I think he was ashamed of himself, because I sensed that he was trying to disassociate himself a little bit from what he was asking of me.

I held my ground and said, "Well, I'll have to think about it."

He said, "Okay. You think about it. I'll call you tomorrow."

I left the office knowing full well that I would be heading back to New York within the week, because nothing in the world was more offensive to me than what he was asking. Here I am in a culture that denies me my personhood. I'm taking the Jim Crow car in all trains below the Mason-Dixon line.

I live in a city in which I've been rebuffed at the doors of many restaurants, a city where Josephine Baker gets turned away and barred from fashionable nightclubs. I'm living with the constant reminder that the law of this land once declared me to be three-fifths of a human being, and that only one hundred years earlier the Chief Justice of the U.S. Supreme Court had declared people of my race to be "so inferior, that they had no rights which the white man was bound to respect." Everywhere I look, everywhere I turn, every attempt I make to articulate myself as otherwise is met with resistance, and here this guy is saying to me, "We want you to swear your loyalty."

To what I wanted to know.

Okay, I went back to rehearsal and Richard Brooks asked me what had happened.

I said, "Nothing." I said, "The guy's gonna call me tomorrow."

Brooks didn't say anything more, and the next day I went in to work, and there'd been no phone call. The third day I went to work, rehearsing, getting ready, and still there was no phone call.

The day the shooting started, I said to Richard, "You know, I haven't heard from that guy, but I gotta tell you what he wants from me. And I gotta tell you there's no way. He wants my soul." And I was struggling to explain how this was a question of my integrity. I said, "I have to let him know there's no deal makeable here. This is not something that's for sale."

And Richard Brooks looked me in the eye, and he said, "You know what? Fuck him." And we started shooting the picture.

I've always wondered, Did Richard say something to the studio? Did he say, "You're forcing me to find another person on such short notice; I can't do it, and it's gonna cost me to delay, and it's gonna cost the studio money"?

I don't know what he said, or if indeed he said anything. Maybe the guy himself began to say, "Jesus Christ, what am I doing here?"

Whatever happened, all I know for sure is that I never heard from that guy again.

Not long after I finished that movie, I was back in New York, and I got a call from David Susskind, the television producer. He said, "I've got a script that's just the greatest, and I want you to play it." He sent it to me and it was fabulous, something called *A Man Is Ten Feet Tall*. I loved the title; it really spoke to what the movie was about.

I told David, "I love it. I want to do it."

He said, "Great, we got a deal."

We were just about to go into rehearsal, no contracts yet, when I got a call from an NBC guy who said, "Could you come in?" So I went in to see him, and again he gave me this form to sign. It was a loyalty oath, and once again it made a point of asking me to disassociate myself from this man I so greatly admired, Paul Robeson.

Well, at this point I couldn't hold back what was inside. I didn't permit it to explode, you know? I was much more in control than that, but I couldn't hide my feelings. I told him that the man he was talking about was a man I respected a great deal, and yes I knew him, and yes I liked him. I liked the fact that he was a stand-up guy. He was a good person to me, I said, and I could not and would not, under any circumstances, be a party to anything that denigrated him.

To sum it all up I said, "Thank you very much, but no thanks," and I left.

I called David Susskind, and I told him what the situation was, and he said, "Let me have a go at this."

I said, "Fine." But I went on to explain that I simply couldn't do this. I knew all about the rightwing, leftwing tug-of-war stuff. I was perfectly capable of interpreting it on the basis of how it affected me as a young black man in America. My political awareness had matured by then. Yes, I was definitely, by then, inclined toward the left of center. Yes, there I found more people like Phil Rose and David Susskind, people demonstrating a genuine willingness to receive me as an equal. This was reason enough, I suppose, for the FBI to keep an eye on me, given the fear and panic of those terrible cold war days of madness. A time in which a young, African-American male was at odds with his times and in constant search for answers to the core conflicts in his life. Conflicts that had little or nothing to do with politics and everything to do with the cultural forces rooted inside him and the multitude of daily surrenders demanded of him by their social surroundings. Balance is what he was looking for, but he hadn't yet learned its name. In time he will come to know it as a state of being. It can only be found at a place that is widely believed not to exist. Truth is that there is a place of space that does exist between two opposites everywhere, and somewhere therein dwells a point at which balance can be found.

The people who were kind to me were kind to me, you know? If I had dug into their motives, I might have found that they were politically different from me, or maybe politically in tune with me. Yes, I knew liberals and progressives and Democrats and Republicans and fellow travelers, communists, anarchists, Bolsheviks, Trotskyites; but whatever they were was their choice—and they were free to so choose.

Blacklist or no, I was determined that I was going to be an actor, because I felt a deep connection between myself and the craft. And blacklist or no, I swore I'd find jobs, or I'd work in a little theater, I'd work in off-Broadway theater, I'd work in Harlem, I'd work as a porter or janitor or wherever I could find jobs. To support my family, I would go out and work as a carpenter's helper if need be, which I did.

I was fine working in the little restaurant and washing my dishes and putting on the barbecue and selling it for eighty cents a meal. I would far rather wash dishes and work over a grill any day than sign a loyalty oath I considered repugnant.

But some weeks later I received a call from David Susskind and he said to me, "I want to go into rehearsal."

I said, "David, what do you mean? I told you I can't sign that thing."

He said, "Listen, I think these guys are nuts. Let's just go into rehearsal and see."

So we started in and we did that play, and it was a bombshell. The story was about this guy working on the docks, the only black guy in the gang. And a white kid drifts on, a kid from the South, and he gets hired and put in the same gang that I'm in, and he turns out to be a wonderful kid with a remarkably philosophical outlook on life. He and I become very close friends, to the chagrin of the bad guys. It was like a morality play. It was a wonderful presentation on television, and later we did it as a film. It was called *Edge of the City* on the big screen.

For the television show, which aired October 21, 1955, on NBC, the part of my wife was played by a young actress named Hilda Simms. She was a very fair-complected African-American woman who had become a star on Broadway playing Anna Lucasta. Her complexion was so fair that on the black-and-white television screens of the day she looked white.

Well, when we went on the air that evening, the switchboard at NBC lit up; it was jammed, you hear me when I tell you? I mean *jammed.* Jammed from the first scene throughout the whole teleplay, which ran for an hour, live television, a Philco Playhouse presentation. The Philco people were deluged with letters as well, people writing about this being such a scandal. Such an issue.

The critics thought the piece was excellent, but the country just wasn't used to it.

The wonderful irony, of course, is that Hilda Simms *was* black—just not black enough to suit the country's perception at that moment.

The curious thing about being an outsider is that you never know where your guardian angels are lurking. Had that studio guy called back, I would have said, "Hey, I can't oblige you. What you want me to do is sign away my loyalty. You're fucking with my dignity." Had he called back and I'd said that to him, I wouldn't have gotten work at MGM, you follow? And the guy at NBC. When I said, "No, I'm outta here" and left, did that guy say to David, "Look, I talked to the kid, and he didn't give much, but listen, what are we doing here? Why don't you go ahead and make your movie." Again, I don't know what happened. All I know for sure is that whatever list I was on that prompted these encounters with studio and network attorneys didn't in the end have any discernible effect on my career.

By the same token, these were the days of the big studio contracts. In *Blackboard Jungle*, the kid who played the bad guy, Vic Morrow, was offered a contract at MGM. All the other guys were talking about who else was being considered for a contract. But it never entered my mind that there was a chance of that for me. The great good fortune in that situation is that I never *was* considered, because had I been considered, the temptation would have been to accept. That's guaranteed salary, you know? I probably would have wound up on suspension more often than not, because I probably wouldn't have done the stuff they offered me. But by remaining an outsider on the free market, I was able to pick and choose my projects, which led to work I can still stand behind, work informed by my life experience, work aligned with my values.

In 1955 I was sent to Atlanta to do publicity for *Blackboard Jungle*. I went down primarily to do black newspapers and black radio. When I was done, I was at the airport, ready to leave, but I was hungry and decided to have a bite. So I went to a very nice restaurant, where all the waiters were black; the maître d' himself, dressed in a tuxedo, was black. He recognized me, I suppose, from some movie.

I appeared at the entrance to this restaurant, and he said, "May I help you?"

I said, "Yes, I'd like a table."

I saw his eyes widen a bit. "Are you alone?" he asked.

I said, "Yes."

He said, "Mr. Poitier, I'm sorry. I could give you a table, but we're going to have to put a screen around you."

And I said to him, I said, "What do you mean?"

"Well, it's the practice here; it's the law."

I looked into his eyes, and I could see that he was pained by having to do this. I could tell it; I could smell it. For him, another black man, to be saying, "We do have this table, but we'll have to put a screen around you"—it must have hurt.

So I said, "Well, no thank you," and I walked away feeling for the man. Not feeling for myself, because I was getting out of there. But I was also somewhat impervious, because that wasn't me. The me they saw and wanted to put a screen around didn't exist to me.

But did I feel some outrage? Of course. Did I feel angry? Yes, but I took it in stride—because this moment of absurdity was, in fact, so totally unremarkable. To African-Americans in 1955 this kind of insult was old hat. So I digested it, and I went on with my life to fight other battles, as I had to. But I never accommodated it.

In 1955, if the nation had cared to take an honest look, it would have seen the approaching civil rights storm kicking up dust on the horizon, coming, perhaps, to seek out the young, quiet preacher of the gospel, destined to lead the way across the difficult and painful years ahead. In fact, before 1955 had passed into history, Martin Luther King, Jr.'s, appearance on the national scene seemed to have no end in sight.

FIVE

A PATCH OF BLUE

BRENT STAPLES DID a piece in the *New York Times* not long ago saying that when white kids run amok, it's time for soul-searching in America, time to figure out our ills. But the problems of black kids always remain "other" and somehow apart.

When we did *Blackboard Jungle* there were forces in the country, Clare Booth Luce among them, that described the film as un-American. They thought it was a misrepresentation of American high school education. Well, it certainly wasn't the kind of school that Ms. Luce's kids would have attended. There were a couple of Hispanic kids, some black kids, and *all* the kids were lower-income. It was a vocational school in New

York City, a school for the incorrigibles and the kids who weren't doing too well. The message coming loud and clear from these critics of our film was, "This isn't 'us.'" But Richard Brooks, the film's director, had a different message: "Yes it is. This is 'us' too."

The film's theme had to do with courage and belonging. Those issues were presented within the context of how an ethnically and racially mixed class of hard-knocks kids moved and changed over time. The individuals in that classroom came to certain realizations having to do with self-perception, courage, and the abuse of power. All of these elements were very creatively orchestrated.

Further animating this already lively mix, the producer added rock and roll to the soundtrack! Let me tell you, in the mid-fifties, with my character's alienated and uncooperative presence in that classroom challenging the authority of the teacher (but winding up an ally of his on some level), and with Bill Haley and the Comets singing "Rock Around the Clock"—well, the result was an electric jolt.

Blackboard Jungle was made in 1954, the year of *Brown v. Board of Education*, but that court decision notwithstanding, black schools at that time were invisible to white America. This was the era of the Andrews Sisters and Perry Como in terms of popular entertainment. *Your Hit Parade* was the big show on television, and the big cultural barometer. The sit-ins of the Civil Rights Movement wouldn't begin for quite a few years. In 1954 the issue of race was still damn near unchanged from when I got off the boat in Florida in 1943. Back then I couldn't go into certain stores and try on a pair of shoes. If I wanted something from a restaurant outside the community in which I was confined, I had to go to a back door. If I rode the bus, I was in the back of the bus. If I wanted to take a train, I was in the Jim Crow car. Thurgood Marshall was running around the country bringing suits at various places, but America wasn't ready for change yet. Most folks didn't want to hear the news.

I made 750 dollars a week for *Blackboard Jungle*, and I was overjoyed. That was a monumental amount for me, but still I knew it wasn't going to change my life. I went back to New York, back to Riverside Drive at 147th Street, back to my restaurant empire, which had grown to three establishments, only one of which was profitable. We were on a slide, and before long the whole thing fell apart. When my partner and I dissolved our relationship, he took the one decent location, and I was left with the other two—which also left me at my wits' end. Here I was, a well-known face in the movies, with my only form of consistent income a business that wasn't working, with three children to support and no money.

My father-in-law was a master bricklayer. After a bit of soul-searching I went to him and asked if he could teach me how to lay bricks. My brother-in-law was designated as the teacher. He took me up to 126th Street, to a two-family house with a back-yard owned by a friend of his, and he set me up with a stack of bricks and some cement. It was a tight space, actually, and they got me going with the plumb line and the white string to keep the rows straight. I tried and tried, but I evidently didn't have the knack.

When I got home I told my wife, "Don't worry. I'll get a job." And I meant it. I'd been a carpenter's helper once before. I'd even once had a job stacking barrels of nails. I'd spent a whole day going around to the entrance of the building to get the barrels, then dragging those babies around back to a crawl space under the floor and stacking them in. That was a back-breaker.

Of all my father's teachings, the most enduring was the one about the true measure of a man. That true measure was how well he provided for his children, and it stuck with me as if it were etched in my brain. I didn't know where I was going next, but I knew that failure wasn't an option.

The restaurant was once and for all finito. I went next door to the little newsstand and tobacco shop. I gave the owner all the food that was left over and whatever fixtures he could use, and I closed the doors. I owed back rent, so I had to leave the rest of the equipment. And then I just walked away.

That's when I got the call from Richard Brooks to make *Something of Value* in Kenya. And from there my career really took off.

This was still 1950s America, however, an America in which a career like this had never even been dreamed of for an outsider of color; it had never happened before in the history of the movie business—a black leading man. I was in the midst of a revolutionary process with this institution I was so at odds with. But my eye was still on "the nature of things," not the career. I was only doing what seemed natural to me, but I knew in the larger scheme of things that it was far from "natural," and that it didn't obviate what was going on in everyday America. There was still gross unfairness in jobs all around me, in living space, in the manner in which black Americans were received.

I saw the truth clear as could be. The explanation for my career was that I was instrumental for those few filmmakers who had a social conscience. Men like Darryl Zanuck, Joe Mankiewicz, Stanley Kramer, the Mirisch brothers, Ralph Nelson, Mike Frankowitch, David Susskind—men who, in their careers, felt called to address some of the issues of their day.

With my earnings from *Something of Value* I was able to buy a two-family house in Mt. Vernon, New York, for twenty-seven thousand dollars. We lived in the ground-floor apartment with three kids (and a fourth on the way) in what was a mixed, but mostly black, community. Among our neighbors—an extraordinary bunch—were Ossie Davis and Ruby Dee. It was a middle-class neighborhood made up of people with either solid professions or secure jobs. Ossie, Ruby, and I knew we represented a slight departure from the norm. Black actors earning as much as a middle-class living amounted to less than one percent of all black actors in the profession. The handful of those lucky enough to have employment had to be constantly mindful of the uncertainties attendant to such fragile statistics and keep an eye out in case the winds of fortune should shift unnoticed and blow them back beyond the poverty line. Through training passed down from all the earlier generations who had to be careful where they walked on the sidewalk, we had the radar to pick up vibrations—good and bad—moving in our direction. Especially when threatening situations arose, all judgment calls required clearance by intuition as a court of last resort. Only then would a course of action be determined.

In 1958 I did another picture, *The Defiant Ones*, that took some heat. Here a good portion of the controversy came from my friends in the black community. It was a Stanley Kramer film written by some very intense and committed progressives, based on their own convictions about race in America. The story was about two fugitives from a chain gang, one white and one black, literally bound together—at least at the beginning—who could never maneuver their way safely through the system. Each misunderstood the other, but they also misunderstood their own individual limitations; so they scapegoated each other.

They weren't able to clearly define what class was, what race was. They experienced poverty, but they couldn't objectively characterize it over and above the fact that they didn't have any money in their pockets. They were simply poor, and that pissed them off, and each used the other to justify his anger—until each discovered that the real difficulty was within himself.

Stanley Kramer's message in the film was that all people are fundamentally the same. Our differences are, for the most part, cosmetic. The character played by Tony Curtis demonstrated that the society we'd constructed wasn't too kind to a goodly number of people who weren't black, who weren't Hispanic, who weren't Asian, who weren't Native American. Some of the people being given a tough time were Irish, and some were

Italians, and some were French, and some were Spanish, and some were eastern European. Modern society wasn't too terrific to many of them—at times, to *most* of them.

Greed and cruelty are pretty widely distributed throughout humanity, as are their victims. You can have oppression of one sort or another all across the board culturally speaking, and all across the board racially speaking, and all across the board religiously speaking. The down-and-out characters played by Tony Curtis and me in *The Defiant Ones* weren't willing to give any credence to this commonality until their experience thrust it right up in their faces and they could no longer ignore it. That's why, at the end, they wound up on that railroad trestle, one guy holding the other guy, struggling to survive, hanging on, but singing a song, a song of hope.

They're interchangeable, these two guys. The slight difference—*very* slight difference—of one being white and one being black obscures all the other issues about the nature of society. To lay all of society's ills on racial differences is simplistic.

Nonetheless, there was criticism of *The Defiant Ones*. A small but highly vocal subset of viewers loved the film but took exception to the ending. They were saying, essentially, "We aren't ready for oneness." Only *this* time the sentiment was from the black perspective.

Certain of my friends in the Hollywood community wanted more of a sense of satisfaction from the ending—a payback satisfaction, you follow? The moment that sets up the final scene is when Tony Curtis was unable to run as fast as I had to catch the moving freight train that had become our last chance for escape. He had tried with all his might to reach my out-stretched hand and hold on. At one point, in fact, our hands almost clasped—another inch was all he needed—but then his fingers began to slip away from mine. It was at that moment that I tumbled off the train too, following after him. So what my friends were questioning was whether I should have stayed on the train and said, "Screw that guy." I explained that the scene in question had been clearly designed by the writers and the director to demonstrate that something had happened in the arc of both characters, something powerful enough that my character felt compelled to make that sacrifice, for a *friend*. My adjustment as an actor for playing the scene as written was the thought that maybe we'll get to the bottom of the hill and be able to take off, or the posse might assume we're still on the train. Nevertheless, from the point of view of those friends my character's tumbling off the train added an unsatisfactory note to the tag of the film. People who saw it that way would have let Tony Curtis go to suffer his fate, whatever that was, and they would have stayed on the train. Now, if I'd been in my character's shoes, in real life, what would I have done? Truth is I'm not altogether sure where I would have come down. But as a professional actor my job was to create the character with the sensibility to conduct himself in the way he behaved at the end, and that's exactly how I played him. The movie's point of view was Stanley Kramer's. And I'm very happy to say, now, in ret-rospect, that it was a good choice on his part, and on the writer's part. And indeed on my part for playing the character as it was written. It was a message of tolerance that has stood up pretty well, given that the picture was made over forty years ago.

By the end of the movie the two characters had each made peace with that part of the self that they'd come to terms with in the other. Tony's character was lying there in my arms in bad shape, but making jokes about our situation, and he pulled the whole thing together by saying, in effect, "There's much about you that is me, and there's much about me that is you, and I'm comfortable with that." The movie ended before viewers could question how long this comfort would last or where it would lead or how profound it was. But it seems to me that the kind of realization Tony's character came to doesn't fade. You may ignore it—you may find that it becomes advantageous politically or socially to ignore it later in life—but you can't erase it, because it's an experience that takes root down at the deepest level of commonality—down where all of us were molded out of the same clay.

For myself, I rarely have the desire to stick it to people. It's enough for me to know that I've held myself in good standing with *me*, you see. It's enough for me to be able to look at the film and say, "That represents me well. That's how I would like people to see me. I would like them to see me as a person who has some value unto himself, and there it is."

But when I'm done wrong by someone, I'm not above putting that person on the rack in my mind, you know? I rage against the misdeed by devising all kinds of responses and reactions that would dissipate my anger, but it's all in imaginary form. Then I become sorry for the thoughts and contemplate forgiveness.

In this life of mine I can't recall any situation in which forgiveness hasn't ultimately been the settlement. However, *getting* to forgiveness hasn't necessarily been a rapid transition. Still, I level out with most such relationships at least cleansed of the rancor, if not intact. And I live better with the situation even if a relationship is altered irreparably in some ways.

Governor Wallace, before his death, said he was sorry for what he had done, and he spoke of the harm and the pain his views and actions had caused. Jesse Jackson went to see him, and I think a form of absolution took place. When you genuinely and sincerely apologize for harm and pain, it's a sign that your life has taken you to another place from where you were when you caused the harm and pain and had no apologies to make. But the process is never simple, and words can never undo lives destroyed.

We've been at this game of human history for a long time, and yet in just the past few years we've witnessed hundreds of thousands of people in Rwanda, in Kosovo, in Bosnia, and elsewhere tortured and killed in the name of ethnic differences. We have a history whose centuries are replete with genocide and attempted genocide.

What humanity has perpetrated goes by different names at different times. What began in Central and South America in the name of Ferdinand and Isabella culminated at the Little Bighorn and Wounded Knee. We called it "exploring the New World," but it caused millions of deaths and the absolute elimination of cultures.

Today, maybe the majority of countries aren't involved in such cruelties, but the majority of countries rarely have been.

It's generally one country, and then another, and then maybe a war between three or four countries. So here we are at the dawn of a new millennium, and how much closer are we to the enlightenment that would take us beyond such behavior?

It might very well be that all we're going to get is an opportunity to rail against the darkness, and to hope and dream and imagine and expect that one day our species—in the form of our children, or our grandchildren, or some progeny in generations to come—will arrive at that place.

In 1964 I was awarded the Oscar for best actor for my performance in *Lilies of the Field*, the first African-American so honored. Did I say to myself, "This country is waking up and beginning to recognize that certain changes are inevitable"? No, I did not. I knew that we hadn't "overcome," because I was still the only one. My career was unique in all of Hollywood. I knew that I was a one-man show, and it simply shouldn't be that way. And yet in a way I found the accolade itself quite natural. I wasn't surprised that such good things were happening to me, because I'd never seen myself as less than I am. When I realized that I could be a better than utilitarian actor, I realized that I had the responsibility, not as a black man, but as an artist, to exercise tremendous discipline. I knew the public would take my measure, and that was constantly in my calculations.

By this time my family had moved to a seven-acre estate in Pleasantville, New York, a huge place in a very upscale community where we were treated very well. I remember the ladies who came as a welcoming committee, all white, and told us about the community. Our kids played with their kids, and our kids had no difficulties in the public schools.

In the 1960s and 1970s, I stayed at many of New York City's finest hotels. Always without incident. Treated with respect on every occasion. Likewise in restaurants, stores, theaters, and, of course, all public-supported venues. None of which should be taken to mean that racism wasn't painfully evident in other ways, in other forms. Still, while that great city was no racial paradise, she was, without question, seductive as hell. She was, in addition, a clear-cut improvement over Mississippi.

There was, of course, no city or state that didn't have its atmosphere of racial attitudes. Black artists traveling could still have problems with accommodations, for example—and that, of course, was nothing compared to the struggles of millions of ordinary black folks in this country who were having a very hard time. Love for Duke Ellington or Nat Cole couldn't obscure the shameful treatment of others.

But it was out of that persistent set of difficult circumstances that the student activists came. It wasn't the artists who carried the day; it was these brave young people who said, "Wait a minute. We've come to the table with all the respect we can muster, and you've done nothing. Now you *will* pay attention to us. How much more you gonna do to us? You can kill us. You can turn dogs on us and beat us, but you'll have to drag us away ten at a time, and there will be hundreds more to take our place."

The country just couldn't fathom it. To many, this upheaval seemed to come out of nowhere, because for such an unbearably long time no attention had been paid to problems of racial inequality.

Sammy Davis, Jr., Duke Ellington, Count Basie, Lena Horne, Sidney Poitier—we weren't leading the charge. We weren't at the forefront, getting our heads cracked open, though our careers were a reflection of what was possible when attention *was* paid. Twenty-five years earlier it hadn't been widely expected, with opportunities so meager, that blacks could be scientists, statesmen, artists. Every time I stepped out, I felt the responsibility to do whatever I could to make pending successes seem a natural expectation.

During the mid-sixties I was approached for another project by Pandro Berman, the filmmaker who had produced *Blackboard Jungle.* Now, ten years later, he wanted to do something called *A Patch of Blue.*

Guy Green was to be the director. An English film editor who had gone into directing and had done some really impressive films, he had fallen in love with this material. I don't recall whether he had brought it to Pandro Berman or Pandro Berman had brought it to him. But when I was approached about a part, I read the script very, very carefully before having a talk with Guy Green as to how he saw the material. Because this was a delicate matter, though a wonderfully original idea—a blinded white girl and a black guy who comes into her life. You know, it was pregnant with all kinds of interesting possibilities, but it was also very tricky in terms of how society would receive it. There were many, many miscarriages that would have to be avoided in order to make something that was not only entertaining but useful.

I came away with the sense that this guy might have a good fix on the subject matter. Why did I feel this way? Was it because he was English? I don't think so, because the English are no less subject to frailties on questions of race than anybody else. But there was a humanity to the guy—I mean, I got really good vibes from him about how he saw the world—so I signed on.

I went to rehearsals in the prefilming preparation period and met a young lady named Elizabeth Hartman. She was a plain-looking, warm, delicate, and apparently fragile person, ideal for the part. I wasn't aware then, when I met her, that she had dressed herself down for the role. She was quite an attractive girl. She was also a well-trained young actress who had developed a strong technique.

We started rehearsing, and I was struck by the magnificent work Elizabeth did. As for myself, I was traveling over ground I had never covered before—you know?—and I was dipping into emotional pockets that were new to me. This was a white girl, and we were in 1960s America. This was a revolutionary attempt at filmmaking, so I was mentally awake in every way. I had my eye out, my ear out, and I was quite primed to make sure that nothing untrue, uncomplimentary, or stereotypical occurred. I wanted to make sure that the story was told with dignity and respect for the questions involved. This wasn't the story of an interracial couple, mind you. This was simply a guy trying to help a young girl who was in need. It was a very human story.

But this was also the time of the March on Selma, the first Civil Rights Act, and the sit-ins. A lot of stressful stuff was coming down. The question of race was rattling the country to its very foundation, so everything in me was on the lookout. I had already predetermined what my character should look like from my point of view. I could be honest to my craft, and I could deliver this character in full. I mean *really* in full, including all of his weaknesses and all of his shortcomings. He would be a human being in total, not a one-dimensional cardboard replica of a human being, as is the case in too many movies— particularly movies about racial questions in America.

I couldn't control how the rest of the movie would go. I didn't know how Shelley Winters was going to sketch the character of the girl's mother, for example. It was none of my business. I could raise objections only if I saw something that struck me as totally off the mark. But Shelley was a professional, and not only did she bring to bear all the shortcomings of that character, all the prejudices of that character, all the imperfections of that character; she added more. And the *more* she added included character details of a fairly despicable person, but none of the characteristics were completely foreign to other human beings as well.

The part of my brother was played by Ivan Dixon, a tremendous actor. He sculpted that part beautifully, so that all the things I wanted to come out of the sequences between the two of us, Dixon and myself, they just flowed. And then there were, of course, peripheral characters, such as Elizabeth Hartman's grandfather.

So everyone in the cast was doing super-duper work. And then, about a third of the way through, I really tuned in to where the director was coming from, and I relaxed completely. I knew that I was in good hands. I knew that his take on the material was such that he was going to be absolutely faithful to the story, but he was also going to be absolutely faithful to the humanity that was implied in the story.

I'm not always satisfied with my work in every scene in every picture. But in *A Patch of Blue* I was coming from a different place, and the performance, by my measurement, was absolutely on target; and I felt that all the way through. Much of this had to do with what I was getting from the other actors. They really kept me reaching for something that I hadn't even been aware was in me. I saw the movie, and by God, it was a *picture*, a performance that was better than I thought I could manage.

I mean, it was *good work*. The actors around me were really cooking, and much of their brilliance reflected on my performance, whether it was deserved or not. It *had* to reflect on my performance because I was the central character with this girl, and how things were with me and her, collectively and individually, was what those other characters were about.

I played a likable guy. I played a good, decent, useful human being—and mind you, much of what was being made in Hollywood at that time, with very rare exceptions, wasn't complimentary from the black perspective. It was a proud moment for me, especially when I thought back to Butterfly McQueen, Stepin Fetchit, Hattie McDaniel, and Mantan Moreland.

The Hollywood of an earlier day had made questionable use of such fabulous talents as Lena Horne and Rex Ingram and Ethel Waters—talents that were never given the respect of a truly objective evaluation. I mean, these were *actors*. I had been introduced to many of them when I was a youngster starting out. I had met Louise Beavers. I knew something of Mantan Moreland; I had met the man. I knew Rex Ingram, Bill Walker, Juanita Moore. I knew so many of those people. I had met them and found them three-dimensional human beings. Some were articulate, some were very ordinary in their speech patterns, some were quite erudite, some were just plain interesting people—but they all were reduced by the requirements of a racist society and an industry that knew how to reflect the society racially in only that one way. I mean, there were no parts for black schoolteachers, for example. And if there were schoolchildren, they were all pickaninnies with their hair combed upwards as if their scalp had been electrified, and giggling and rolling their eyes like Buckwheat in the *Our Gang* comedies.

Back in Los Angeles, in the bowels of the film industry, these people were close at hand, right over there in West Los Angeles toward the Central Avenue area, Adams area, Crenshaw area. And I saw the dignified homes they lived in, and I was in some of those homes, and I gotta tell you, it had to have been some massive negative attitude operative in society (and, consequently, in this industry) to characterize a people without the slightest acknowledgment of their humanity anywhere evident.

These artists were very much like the black actors and actresses I know today, only they were chained to stereotypes when many of them had the wherewithal to soar. They simply got no chance. They lived and died, lived and died, never having had an opportunity to express their genuine talent.

I'm not racially sensitive to the point that I want to foist untruths on my history. As a matter of fact, I'm more inclined to critically examine that which I know to be the truth. So when I look at my history through the black actors and actresses who preceded me, I need to be fair to those actors and actresses, but I also need to be fair to the society, you know? What good did the participation of blacks in the movie industry do for the actors and actresses who represented their race, and *to* those actors and actresses. What *harm* did it do to them and to generations unborn? I put all that in the mix, and even so, all I can conclude is that Hollywood was a really insensitive place when it came to black people.

We needed alternatives. In New York City there were people like Oscar Micheaux, a black man making movies there—but he had to put the finished product under his arm and go around from place to place to find cinema houses for black people, and there weren't very many of those. He was on the road all the time. Whenever he finished a picture, he went off traveling, putting his work in black theaters. He has become a kind of a father figure for the current black filmmakers in America, though of course they know of him only through the legend of what he did.

There were other black film personalities making black pictures. There was a guy named Ralph Cooper in New York, who was a very, very big film personality. He was an actor who played all kinds of parts, including romantic parts and gangster parts. There was even Herb Jeffries, the black singing cowboy.

The studios wouldn't go near that kind of stuff in those days. So Mantan Moreland, Stepin Fetchit, Butterfly McQueen, and Hattie McDaniel—they could only dream of a time when there would be a Denzel Washington, a Wesley Snipes, an Angela Bassett, a Will Smith, a Samuel L. Jackson, and a Morgan Freeman, when there would be an invention called television to harbor a legend named Bill Cosby. They would have to stretch their imagination pretty far to be able to dream in those terms.

So I look back on those people who came before me, and I owe them a debt, you know? Yes, sometimes I squirmed when I watched what they had to do. Sometimes I applauded when something they did really touched my heart. But I knew when I came on the scene how painful it had to have been for them sometimes. Certainly not all the time, but sometimes it had to have been a bitch for them to say some of those words and behave in some of those ways. So I look back on them with respect and appreciation. They were our predecessors, and they endured. They were the ones that life and nature and history required to walk that road.

They gave birth to me, because a part of what I do, a part of what Denzel Washington does, a part of what Angela Bassett does is to respectfully reflect on the endurance of those people. We were, and are, as they would have wished to be, but we could not be as we are without their having paid a price.

SIX

WHY DO WHITE FOLKS LOVE SIDNEY POITIER SO?

NINETEEN SIXTY-EIGHT was a time of incredible conflict and contrast. It was the year when both Martin Luther King, Jr., and Robert F. Kennedy were assassinated, the year Lyndon Johnson succumbed to the cultural clashes over Vietnam and gave up the presidency, the year of the police riot at the Democratic National Convention in Chicago. But for me personally it was also a year of tremendous professional satisfaction. I had the number one box office success, as well as numbers two and three: *To Sir, with Love*, with Lulu and Judy Geeson; *In the Heat of the Night*, with Rod Steiger and Lee Grant; and *Guess Who's Coming to Dinner*, with Spencer

Tracy and Katharine Hepburn. And I think we did work that has more than stood the test of time.

Yet given the quickly changing social currents, there was more than a little dissatisfaction rising up against me in certain corners of the black community, a cultural wave that would crest a few years later when the *New York Times* published an article titled "Why Do White Folks Love Sidney Poitier So?"

The issue boiled down to why I wasn't more angry and confrontational. New voices were speaking for African-Americans, and in new ways. Stokely Carmichael, H. Rap Brown, the Black Panthers. According to a certain taste that was coming into ascendancy at the time, I was an "Uncle Tom," even a "house Negro," for playing roles that were nonthreatening to white audiences, for playing the "noble Negro" who fulfills white liberal fantasies. In essence, I was being taken to task for playing exemplary human beings: the young engineer turned schoolteacher in *To Sir, with Love*, the Philadelphia homicide detective far from home in *In the Heat of the Night*, and the young doctor who comes courting the daughter of Tracy and Hepburn in *Guess Who's Coming to Dinner*.

Now, admittedly, the young teacher I portrayed was the epitome of virtue. Elegant and well-spoken, intelligent and kind, he was also courageous and steadfast as he stood up to abuse and maintained his commitment to the students under his charge. Police Detective Tibbs, likewise, was a man of great courage and intelligence, as well as admirable restraint. And the young doctor in *Guess Who's Coming to Dinner*—aside from being a charming suitor, an exceedingly courteous guest, and a paragon of a son—had academic credentials a mile long and spent his time saving mankind for the World Health Organization.

So the question being raised was, What's the message here? That black people will be accepted by white society only when they're twice as "white" as the most accomplished Ivy League medical graduate? That blacks must pretend to be something they aren't? Or simply that black society does—of course—contain individuals of refinement, education, and accomplishment, and that white society—of course—should wake up to that reality?

The heated tempers of that time have long since cooled, and ideological fashions have come and gone. But the fact remains that in the late sixties civil disobedience gave way to more radical approaches. The angry "payback" of the black exploitation film was just around the corner, and my career as a leading man in Hollywood was nearing its end.

Even so, I think it's all too easy for anyone not a participant in the cultural clashes of that era to unfairly dismiss films such as *Guess Who's Coming to Dinner*, forgetting just how revolutionary they were in the context of their times.

This was another Stanley Kramer picture, of course, and he's the kind of filmmaker who has always asked, "What can I do that will be daring, interesting, and necessary?" In 1967, when he had me read the script for *Guess Who's Coming to Dinner*, I was very impressed. Stanley knew that the country wasn't ready for this one, but his attitude was—well, we're going to do it anyway.

One sign of the times was that he decided not to tell the folks at Columbia Pictures what the movie was about initially, and for good reason. He had a production deal with them for a certain number of pictures, so (for a while, at least) it was enough for him to say that he was going to make the next one with Spencer Tracy, Katharine Hepburn, and Sidney Poitier. But that's *all* he told them.

"Sounds great," they said. "Go ahead and develop the script."

And so he did. But after a certain point he had to go to Columbia again, and he said, "We're really okay. We've come a long way, and I would just like to start putting this thing together."

And they said, "Okay, now let's get this straight. It's Poitier and Tracy and Hepburn, and we're doing this movie. But what's it about?"

"Family stuff," he said. "You know, this is family stuff."

And the guys at Columbia nodded, and Stanley said, "It's gonna be warm, it's gonna be human, and it's gonna be—" whatever. He still didn't really lay it out.

But after a certain point, before the serious money was committed, the folks at Columbia had to see the script; they really had to know what they were buying.

So Stanley said, "Look, I've got these three people. I've got Tracy and Hepburn. Do you know what that combo is? Do you know what that means?" And he's selling, and he's telling them they're running out of chances to get this team, because Tracy isn't a young man. But the fact is once they got their hands on the script, they really didn't want to go down that road. They felt that the subject was simply too much for an American audience, and they felt that the risks were too great.

So they were squirming and they were dodging, and finally someone came up with what Columbia thought could be the loophole in their commitment. Tracy's health prevented the studio from getting him insurance coverage for the production. Legend has it that they tried to use that as an excuse for halting production, but then Tracy refused to take any salary until the film was over, which undercut that argument. So, reluctantly, they acquiesced and let the picture proceed.

Here's the story of how I was taken to Miss Hepburn's house so she could check me out. When I arrived at her door and that door opened, she looked at me and didn't say a word and didn't crack a smile. But that was her M.O. After the longest while she said, "Hello, Mr. Poitier," and I said, "Hello, Miss Hepburn," and the conversation began. I could tell that I was being sized up every time I spoke, every response I made. I could imagine a plus and a minus column, notations in her mind. That's how big a step this was for her, at least to my mind.

After that first meeting, Stanley took me to Tracy's house on Doheny Drive for a little dinner party with the two of them and some other guests. This time Miss Hepburn was much more natural and at ease, but it was still obvious that I was under close observation by both of them.

The truth of the matter is that the formation of this business relationship was almost a literal "pre-enactment" of the situation in the film we were about to make. The black man was coming for dinner, and we didn't usually do that. Now mind you, these were good, enlightened, liberal people. These were major Hollywood stars putting their ideals to the test—but even for them, the fact still remained that "we don't usually do that." They were going to enter into an intense creative partnership with a black man—a partnership in which they would take on one of the primal taboos of our culture, interracial marriage—and "we don't usually do that," either.

Should I have felt condescended to by all the scrutiny from Tracy and Hepburn? Should I have been angry and confrontational? After all, they'd had ample opportunity to know my work. At that time I'd made over thirty films and had won the Oscar for best actor a few years earlier. If it had been Paul Newman they were going to do a movie with, would they have checked him out so thoroughly? But the fact of the matter is I'm not Paul Newman. If Paul had played the part of the young doctor coming to marry their daughter, there would have been no drama.

Having done A Patch of Blue, I had already crossed this societal boundary, but the culture at large, even the liberal and enlightened subculture, had not. Spencer Tracy and Katharine Hepburn were exceedingly decent people, and I think their politics were sound, but I still think asking them to be any more "liberated" in the America that we knew at that time would have been expecting a hell of a lot too much.

So I gave them the benefit of the doubt; I looked at them as ordinary, decent folks. And in fact they turned out to be that—

and a hell of a lot more. But they were anxious early on, for good reason, and they simply had to find out about me.

Spencer Tracy and Katharine Hepburn, like most of their audience, lived in America. More important, they lived in Hollywood, and in their hometown the intrusion of an African-American suitor wasn't a part of the daily practice of the hundreds of marriages that they were privy to in their lives and on the screen.

If they had known twenty-five or thirty black people, ten of whom were actors, three of whom were doctors, four of whom were maids, six of whom were schoolteachers, and some of whom were workaday people, then they would have come to the question informed on a certain level. But being Americans of the middle class or higher, the only black people they would have encountered were, for the most part, the servants in their home and at the studios—blacks who attended Miss Hepburn in whatever ways she required. And as for Mr. Tracy, he struck me as a very human guy who, if given the chance, would come down every time on the side of decency and fairness for all. Now, maybe I thought that in part because of the memorable role he played in *Bad Day at Black Rock*, in which he was wonderfully compassionate to a character played by a black actor named Juano Hernandez. I do know that they were demonstrably *independent* people. While I don't know what the design of their social life was, I doubt that either one of them had ever had all that much social contact with people of color.

Obviously, Tracy and Hepburn knew Stanley Kramer; in fact, Tracy was Kramer's favorite actor. The two men had worked together on *Inherit the Wind*, *Judgment at Nuremberg*, and *It's a Mad Mad Mad Mad World*. Thus Tracy and Hepburn were obliged to bring to bear on me the kind of respect they had for Kramer, and they had to say to themselves (and I'm sure they did), This kid has to be pretty okay, because Stanley is nuts about working with him.

As for my part in all this, all I can say is that there's a place for people who are angry and defiant, and sometimes they serve a purpose, but that's never been my role. And I have to say, too, that I have great respect for the kinds of people who are able to recycle their anger and put it to different uses.

On the other hand, even Martin Luther King, Jr., and Mahatma Gandhi, who certainly didn't appear angry when they burst upon the world, would never have burst upon the world in the first place if they hadn't, at one time in their lives, gone through much, much anger and much, much resentment and much, much anguish.

Anguish and pain and resentment and rage are very human forces. They can be found in the breasts of most human beings at one time or another. On very rare occasions there comes a Gandhi, and occasionally there comes a Martin Luther King, Jr., and occasionally there comes a guy like Paul Robeson or a guy like Nelson Mandela. When these people come along, their anger, their rage, their resentment, their frustration—these feelings ultimately mature by will of their own discipline into a positive energy that can be used to fuel their positive, healthy excursions in life.

It wasn't imaginary circumstances or vicarious experiences

that engendered harsh emotions in the men I've named. It was real situations, for them and for the people around them. But they had some manna, some mechanism, some strength, some discipline, some vision that allowed them to convert that anger into fuel. Anger is negative energy—a destructive force—but they converted it into fuel, into *positive* energy. Their transformed anger fueled them in positive ways; in each case that's exactly what happened.

Nelson Mandela—you think he loved the apartheid practitioners? Oh, no. You think he loved the guys who sentenced him to death and then put him on a rockpile, promising him that he would work there for six months, and left him working there for *thirteen years*, ruining his legs and his knees? Went in a robust prizefighter in the best of physical condition, and they worked him till his feet and ankles suffered lasting damage. But he came out of prison with a respect for himself, for his values, for his cause, and no hatred for the men and women who had spent a commensurate part of their lives trying to destroy him. He resented or disliked or hated what they *represented*, but he was human enough to see them, frailties and all, as human beings. As did Martin Luther King, Jr., who said as much. As did Gandhi, who said as much.

Well, I certainly don't live this ideal every day, but I believe in it with my whole being. If I were asked for an evaluation of myself, I would readily admit to my sins, such as they are, to my weaknesses, my frailties, my shortcomings. I do that all the time, and the reason I can do that and not be ashamed is that I'm willing almost always to try my best. And when I fall short of my reach for something after having tried my best—even when I fall so short that my attempt winds up in sinful behavior—or when my weaknesses tug at my ankles, I accept that. I mean, I accept that failing, but I *can't* accept my sinfulness, my weaknesses, my frailties *unless* I've really tried to reach above them.

Wherever there's a configuration in which there are the powerful and the powerless, the powerful, by and large, aren't going to feel much of anything about this imbalance. After a while the powerful become accustomed to experiencing the power to their benefit in ways that are painless. It's the air they breathe, the water they swim in.

The powerless, who *aren't* swimming in that comfort and that ease, look at the inequity quite differently than the guy across town who's in the comfort seat. But that goes for Japanese and Chinese, that goes for African-Americans and white Americans, that goes for Native Americans and white Americans, that goes for Hispanic Americans and white Americans. It goes for the British and their colonial possessions, many of which are now called commonwealth countries. However much prodding they get from the powerless or the disenfranchised or the slaves, those in power just aren't inclined toward introspection or remorse.

If we examine our own history, we see quite clearly how long it took before there was any acknowledgment of the inequities in our society. Through most of the history of film, we were making movies, for Christ's sake, where the Indians were all bad guys.

When you're addressing power, don't expect it to crumble willingly. If you're going to say, "Hey now, look you guys, please look at what you did and look at yourselves and punish yourselves and at least try to square this thing, right?"—well, you'll make slower progress at that than you would expect. I mean, even the most modest expectations are going to be unfulfilled.

Think about it. Today there are still people all over the world who maintain that the Holocaust didn't happen. There are people in the United States—people among that power echelon we speak of—who maintain that all slaves were happy. There are those power symbols that always say, "Well, it was for the good of the states. It was for the cohesion of the political process." There are myriad justifications for denial.

There are also people who say, "Hey, after thirty years of affirmative action, they've got it made. Black people—it's their own fault if they can't make it today."

Yeah, well, *of course* they say that. And they say it not just about black people. They say it in every country. We did something for you people, whoever "you" are. And we think that's quite enough now.

That's the gist of it: we've done something, and we think it's enough. It may not be perfect, but it damn sure comes close to being okay. Now let us hear you applaud that for a little while. And thank us. And you can take that hat off your head when you come in here thanking us.

That's the way it is. But let's not get stuck there. We have miles to go before we sleep. We have lots to do, and some things just aren't going to get done, you know?

A lot of black leaders, along with a lot of sympathetic white people, would say it's too early in this country for forgiveness. We haven't dealt with accountability yet, admission of guilt yet. And we certainly don't have equality yet. But among the things that we must try to get done is the nurturing of a civilized, fair, principled, humane society. Now, if a part of that nurturing—part of the movement toward it, some of the efforts spent in that direction—would bring us to a new understanding, a new acceptance, even some forgiveness, what then? And not just forgiveness from the people who've been wronged. Forgiveness works two ways, in most instances. People have to forgive themselves too. *The powerful have to forgive themselves for their behavior.* That should be a sacred process.

Compassion for other human beings has to extend to the society that's been grinding the powerless under its heel. The more civilized the society becomes, the more humane it becomes; the more it can see its own humanity, the more it sees the ways in which its humanity has been behaving inhumanly. This injustice of the world inspires a rage so intense that to express it fully would require homicidal action; it's self-destructive, destroy-the-world rage. Simply put, I've learned that I must find positive outlets for anger or it will destroy me. I have to try to find a way to channel that anger to the positive, and the highest positive is forgiveness.

Put simply, I've learned that I must find positive outlets for anger or it will destroy me. There is a certain anger: it reaches such intensity that to express it fully would require homicidal

My father, Reginald Poitier.   My mother, Evelyn.

On a visit to Cat Island.

In the army, 1943.

In my zoot suit.

My "headshot" for *Blackboard Jungle*, 1954.

With Glenn Ford in *Blackboard Jungle*, 1955.

With John Cassavetes in *Edge of the City*, 1957.

Raisin in the Sun with Claudia McNeil, 1961.

With Lilia Skala in *Lilies of the Field*, 1963.

With Tony Curtis in *The Defiant Ones*, 1966.

To Sir, With Love, 1967.

In the Heat of the Night with Rod Steiger, 1967.

Guess Who's Coming to Dinner, 1968

rage—self-destructive, destroy-the-world rage—and its flame burns because the world is so unjust. I have to try to find a way to channel that anger to the positive, and the highest positive is forgiveness.

When I was barely sixteen, still back in Miami, late one night I was stranded in a white, middle-class neighborhood. I had gone to the dry cleaners in "our" part of town, only to discover that my clothes weren't yet ready. This was a major problem for me, because it was already late afternoon and I was planning to leave town the next day. The cleaners told me that I could try to pick up my stuff at the dry-cleaning plant across town. So I took the bus across town to this plant, but my clothes *still* weren't ready. Compounding the problem, by then the buses had stopped running and there I was, left high and dry and extremely out of place.

I focused my attention on passing cars heading in the general direction of "colored town." Whenever I saw one that appeared to have black occupants, I would then—and only then—raise a hitchhiking thumb in the hope of flagging a ride. The first vehicle to stop was the unmarked police car that I had mistakenly thought to contain a black family.

I knew I was in trouble when the window on the front passenger side rolled down and the cop sitting there pointed to his right and said, "See that alley over there, boy? Get your ass up in there. Now." After a quick assessment of the situation, something inside me assumed a steadying control and I complied. The unmarked police car then rolled into the alley behind me.

There was no one else around. Whatever happened, there would be no witnesses. When I turned back around, I saw the muzzle of a revolver sticking through the open rear window on the driver's side, pointed at my head. Through that open window I could hear the dialogue inside the vehicle: "What should we do with this boy?" "Find out what he's doing over here." "Should we shoot him here?" I could see that the hammer of the gun was cocked, and I was scared out of my mind—but mad too, furious at what appeared to be their need to belittle me.

I told them about taking the bus to the dry-cleaning plant, about trying to get my stuff, but the talk in the car only got meaner as the questioning intensified. The officer behind the wheel said, "Boy, if we let you go, you think you can walk all the way home without looking back once?"

"Yes, sir," I replied.

"Think about it now," he challenged. "'Cuz if you look back, just once, we gonna shoot you. Think you can do that?"

"Yes, sir," I reassured him.

"All right, you go ahead now. We'll be right behind you."

I exited the alley, turned right onto the main street, and proceeded to walk the next fifty blocks—never once looking back. By shifting my eyes, but not my head, ever so slightly to the right, I could see that police car reflected in the plate-glass windows I passed. The cops were there, right on my tail, and there they stayed for the entire fifty blocks, until I turned the corner to the place where I was living with my relatives. At that point they sped away.

Fifty blocks is a long time to think about what's happening to you, to stew in the insane injustice of it all. But it's also a good long time to internalize messages such as discipline, independence, the value of character, and toughness of mind.

I've seen reports on the news about parents whose children were murdered, and these parents sought out the murderers to get to know them and try to help them, which is astounding until you think it through. In essence, what else *could* they do? Sure, they could take revenge, destroy the world. But that's the worst hurt a person could have: to see his or her child *senselessly* murdered. So there are people who find a way to turn even that horrible, destructive energy into something positive.

It comes down to changing the way you look at a particular injustice. The parents whose child has been murdered seek to understand the murderer and to go in and try to salvage whatever is salvageable in human terms—in this particular case, a kernel of goodness in the murderer. Well, the parents don't arrive there three days after the child has been murdered, nor do they arrive there some weeks after they've buried their child. They go through what's probably an unbearable hell, because striving for control within them are the various human forces that command us: hatred, anger, fear, a sense of revenge. All of those forces have to play out individually and in groups and sometimes in juxtaposition one to the other.

And when those parents are unable to find easy answers, they have to face their pain. It's when they do that—somewhere in that confrontation—that they may find some suggestion, some indication, some hint, some intuition that will lead them toward looking at the circumstances differently. And one day, one moment, one minute, one second somewhere along the line, they're going to realize that there's no way for them to live with the requirements of their anger, with the requirements of their rage, with the requirements of their hatred. They have to find peace, because they won't get any peace from rerunning those emotions. Somewhere along the line, I guess, out of nature's inexplicable ways, they stumble on a light (or they consciously arrive at that light, or it comes from someplace unknown), and the seed of forgiveness is illuminated.

Did I always have that peace? No. Wasn't I an angry young man when I played the teenager in *Blackboard Jungle?* Certainly I was a different young man when I was nine or ten, and when I was twelve or fifteen, and when I was twenty-seven. So how did I deal with my rage? I dealt with it in ways that were shaped by my early life, my family surroundings, my friends, the fact that I was a member of the black community that was indeed the majority of people in the country. All those things interplayed with each other over my early years to put a certain kind of youngster on that boat heading for Florida in 1943. And when that kid got to Florida and Florida said, "Oh, wow! Let's sit this kid down and tell him, or show him, or explain to him what the rules are," it was too late. You see, by then I had already fashioned my own rules—rules quite contrary to what Florida was then saying to me.

That rage wasn't given very fertile ground in my early, early years on Cat Island and then in Nassau. It was well in its formative stages in the Bahamas, but it never came to the kind of fruition it did in Florida. Florida was in-your-face stuff. Florida was asking you who you were, and you were telling Florida who you were, and then Florida said to you, "No, that's not who you are. *This* is who you are, and *this* is who you will be." And I said no, and the more Florida said yes, the more that fed my rage.

I didn't try to grab a gun from one of the cops and have a shootout with them in that alley in Miami, because that wasn't my nature. That would have been self-destructive. My rage would have destroyed me. The sense of survival I had learned on Cat Island served me well.

Social movement doesn't come all at once, just as it doesn't come out of nowhere. There are moments when it captures the news, like the National Guard in Little Rock, and then we don't hear anything about it nationally for a year, two years, three years, four years, five years—and then *wham!* So much happened in the ten-year period between making *The Defiant Ones* and making *Guess Who's Coming to Dinner, In the Heat of the Night,* and *To Sir, with Love* that when you look at the first picture set against the latter three, it's as if, culturally, far more time than a decade had gone by.

A filmmaker such as Stanley Kramer was an artistic wedge during that period, but art doesn't solve social problems. It's a reminder, it's an irritant, it clarifies, it focuses, but it doesn't *solve.* Potential solutions were ignored until America was forced to confront them. Thurgood Marshall went all over the country in pursuit of solutions, and he sometimes had to dodge Klansmen on his way from court to the airport, or travel from town to town at night, or go home unannounced, or be picked up at railroad stations by patriots in darkened automobiles who sought to protect him. And hard as the NAACP tried, that fearsome anti-solution activity very seldom reached the newspapers. The NAACP had, by that time, become an irritant. It was just, "Oh, those people, they're having problems. They're complaining again."

But something was brewing among the students, and that began to catch on in the late fifties and then take tenacious hold in the early sixties. When they started sitting in, it was small, and they were way ahead of the country. The country was reading about their activity in little bits of coverage that slowly began to appear in the newspapers. Finally they said, "Oh, my God, what's happening here?" As if suddenly someone were creating a crisis. As if this civil disobedience were out of the blue, with no roots to it.

That's how that began to mushroom, but it wasn't an easy journey. Those ten years between *The Defiant Ones* and *Guess Who's Coming to Dinner* were rough. The government found itself asked to defend the rights of people who were denying the rights of others. The government was placed in the position of decreeing that what was on the statute books in the cities and states was improper and defied the Constitution. And the young black students were saying no to the status quo very vocally, and they were laying themselves on the line.

There was turmoil, but there was progress as well. But then Vietnam sidetracked some of that progress with new forms of division in the country, and then protest took on a different tone, creating a more violent reaction. There were riots. There were killings. It was like three steps forward, two steps back, at least in terms of the sentiment expressed in *The Defiant Ones*—the feeling that there's more that joins us together than separates us.

But one progressive step that *wasn't* reversed—and the most fundamental change—was the enforcement of the Constitution with regard to suffrage for blacks. But that was a long time coming. You're talking way back to W.E.B. Du Bois. You're going back to historians like John Hope Franklin. You go through men like A. Philip Randolph, the head of the sleeping-car porters. You go through Roy Wilkins. And then you go through artists like Paul Robeson and Langston Hughes and Richard Wright and Ralph Ellison. And there were more extreme views—people like Marcus Garvey, who was so frustrated, who said, "These people are so intractable, they're so bullheaded with their wrong-headedness, let's all go back to Africa. Let's just get out of here."

All of that energy was coming up smack against the written laws of the states, and all of the laws of the states were backed up by the Constitution. And yet whenever you got too close to the truth there, they would say, "But the law says that you're not a full citizen; you're only three-fifths of a human being, and only a full human being can vote. *Only a full human being can vote.*"

That was the kind of world I was asked to reenter when Walter Mirisch came to see me about playing the part of a

Philadelphia police detective accidentally pulled into a murder investigation in a small town in the Deep South.

When I looked over the script that became *In the Heat of the Night*, my primary issue was the character of a local businessman who had enormous influence in the life of that town. At one point the character I played, Detective Tibbs, found it necessary to question this man. The local police chief, played by Rod Steiger, accompanied me, and we drove up to the mansion on a hill. I was very respectful during our conversation, but in time I had to ask the inevitable question—"Where were you on the night of the murder?"—and he hauled off and slapped me. Obviously, as far as he was concerned, I had stepped over the line in suggesting the possibility that he could be in any way clouded by suspicion. So he whacked me across the face.

In the original script I looked at him with great disdain and, wrapped in my strong ideals, walked out. That could have happened with another actor playing that part, but it couldn't happen with me. I could too easily remember that Miami night with the gun pointed at my forehead, that fifty-block march with those guffawing cops in the patrol car behind me. I told the director that the script needed to be changed.

He said, "Well, what do you suggest?"

I said, "I'll tell you what I'll *insist* upon." I said to Walter, "This gentleman of the Old South is acting out of his tradition, where his honor demands that he whack me across the face." And I said, "You want a moment, you want a really wonderful, impressive moment on the screen?" I said, "Shoot this scene so that without a nanosecond of hesitation, I whack him right back across the face with a backhand slap."

Walter said, "I like it."

It turned out to be a very, very dramatic moment in the film.

The town pillar turned to Rod Steiger's police chief and said, "Gillespie, did you see that?" And Steiger said, as only Steiger could say it, "I saw it!" Then the actor who was playing the old man closed the scene. He turned to me and muttered, "There was a time when I could have had you shot."

For me personally, the emotional center of the film was another scene, one in which Chief Gillespie and Detective Tibbs drove past a field of cotton, a beleaguered-looking crew of field hands dragging their cotton sacks between the rows. Gillespie turned to me and said, in effect, "None of that for you, huh?" But the camera recorded my face as I observed these people. For me the actor, as I watched these black men and women picking cotton, my thought was that I knew I was on the right track with the kind of parts I had been insisting on.

From the way it was in my early days in America, to the point at which I was playing a senior detective representing the Philadelphia Police Department, solving a murder mystery in rural Mississippi—that was movement. But the true progress it represented didn't come from unbridled rage any more than it came from polite submission. Progress then and now comes from the collision of powerful forces within the hearts of those who strive for it. Anger and charity, love and hate, pride and shame, broken down and reassembled in an igneous process that yields a fierce resolve.

SEVEN

DESTRUCTION OR RESURRECTION?

THOSE OF US fortunate enough to be in the movie business and to have our faces spread across the screen for many years become slightly iconographic figures, mythic figures, whether we want to be or not. Those who are given the designation "stars" cease to be simply actors and become a part of the collective unconscious, part of the dream fabric of the culture. It's a tremendous responsibility, and one that members of my profession take on with highly varying degrees of success.

There's a mystery to the relationship between life and an individual human personality, and I think the camera sees that mystery. The individual human personality has, bound up inside itself, a connection to all the wonders of the universe.

When an artist is genuinely at work in his craft, he's more fully calling on those connections to the universal.

What does the camera capture when it looks at me? I'll leave that for others to assess. But staring back at that lens from within myself, I feel that so much of what I've otherwise kept hidden is captured and filtered. What emerges on the screen reminds people of something in themselves, because I'm so many different things. I'm a network of primal feelings, instinctive emotions that have been wrestled with so long they're automatic. The things I don't like about myself, the things I *do* like about myself, the things I'm not but I'd like to be, the things I am but don't want others to know about—these are all percolating inside. All these contradictory aspects are the basic me. Courage and cowardice, strength and weakness, fear and joy, love and hate—that's what makes up the actor so that's available to the camera.

The lens sees what it sees; it's entirely neutral in its gaze. It's not looking for my best or my worst, and there's no guarantee that it will capture something truly representative. It can't mirror the self completely, but I do know that it can tell when I'm thinking, and I know that it can tell when there's something I'm trying to hide.

When I play anger in a scene, it's different from when I experience anger in life. Anger in life is so genuine that it's instantaneous. It may be triggered explosively; it may be triggered at a low level and, depending on what follows, then escalate or subside. That's life. If someone slaps my kid and I see it, then I'm ready to take that person apart. Correct? Okay, now the actor who doesn't have a child but must play such a reaction in a film, where does he go for examples of the feeling? Where does he go for as close as he can get to the stuff of that emotion, and how does he access it so instantaneously that it's as if, in fact, it were real life?

He goes to his sense memory. He goes deep inside himself into a place where all his individual sense memories are stored, and that place them connects him with the universe. That connection gives him access to more than just the memory of what anger is like and what unfairness is or other kinds of impositions or slights or offenses that would trigger anger are like. There's a network of intuitions and instincts. I mean, the *raw* instincts—a genuine network of connections of those forces, energies, and awarenesses that drive humanity. The entire result of the actor's life experiences to that point have been collected in that sense memory, and every one of them is registered there, many of them that wouldn't ordinarily be available to the conscious mind. But in acting, a creative moment requires that the actor enter there. And the camera sees that contact with the sense memory. So what it picks up is something that's almost indescribable. Some people call it *presence*, while others say the camera *likes* that actor. Whatever label we apply, the camera sees *something*; it just simply sees it.

On a mundane level you might say that a particular actor has an expressive face. Even when there are no lines being said, you know something's going on in that mind, in that soul. He's just standing there looking off into space, but there's something going on that seems real and alive and genuine.

That's because he's entering that creative place. Or maybe not so much *entering* it as being *receptive* to it. It could be said that this place, unto itself, gives off a sense of its own existence, and it comes through, maybe even unknown to the personality itself. Because a mind is operating. Because a heart is beating in that chest.

————

DURING FIFTY YEARS in Hollywood, trying to learn how to portray life on the screen, I just may have learned a little about life. If that's in fact the case, I must give credit to some excellent teachers and some extraordinary fellow students.

As for the craft itself, I've never worked with a good actor from whom I didn't learn something useful. During the filming of *In the Heat of the Night*, Rod Steiger's work was a constant reminder of how lucky I was that I had found my way to two of the greatest teachers of any era, Paul Mann and Lloyd Richards. I arrived at the door of their workshop in the 1950s with no understanding of "an actor's technique." Before they took me on, I had been a-c-t-i-n-g! Pretending, indicating, giving the *appearance* of experiencing certain emotions, but never, ever really getting down to where real life and fine art mirror each other.

Steiger was a product of the Actors Studio, and his approach to his work fascinated me. His preparation period for a scene was astonishing in its depth. First he explored everything objectively. Then he made *sub*jective everything that he'd found in his *ob*jective exploration. In this final process, he would zero in on his character so completely that for the entire period of making the picture he would speak in the same cadence. Even sitting down to dinner in the evenings. Even on weekends, when we ventured out to a movie or dinner or when we sat around the motel just running our mouths about various things. Working or not, he would remain completely immersed in the character of that southern sheriff. He spoke with the same accent and walked with the same gait, on and off camera. I was astonished at the intensity of his involvement with the character.

Performing well-written scenes from *In the Heat of the Night* with Rod Steiger and Lee Grant was an illuminating experience. Whatever Lloyd Richards and Paul Mann had taught me about technique had fallen snugly into place and allowed me to hold my own, pound for pound, among heavyweights like Steiger and Grant. Throughout the making of that film I sensed that I was on the threshold of discovering what acting really is, which is a way of getting at the core of what *life* really is.

I always knew that first-rate actors had exceptional gifts, but I also knew that an exceptional gift, in and of itself, didn't necessarily a first-rate actor make. It was essential that the actor's gift be subject to a technique, a learned procedure, a discipline, in order for him to constantly function at close to his best. I had fumbled about for years trying to find that "learned procedure," that "discipline." I can't tell you how difficult it was for me to put together all the pieces of an effective technique.

There are things that we don't accept in theater—*won't* accept, *shouldn't* accept in theater—that we *have* to accept in life. Those are what we call *accidents*. Some theatrical accidents happen because actors fail to look at causality. Maybe we should all be questioning cause all the time to see if what it appears to be is what it in fact is. Be aware that even if B appears to follow A all the time, proximity doesn't guarantee causality. But no matter whether we misplace, misread, or misidentify it, there is *always* a cause.

Discovering cause and effect, learning to follow it like a beacon, was a turning point for me. That's when my internal measure as an artist kicked in. Thanks to fine actors like Steiger, Grant, Ruby Dee, Marlon Brando, Alice Childress, Frank Silvera, Spencer Tracy, Canada Lee, and the many others whose examples over the years slowly led me to the light, I was closer than ever to not only being able to recognize the fine line that separates high-quality "indicating" from first-rate organic acting, but also closer myself to successful performances on that side of the line where the real pros worked.

While I wasn't home yet in the truly professional sense, I was a long way from those early times back in the theatrical woods when I was told by fellow inexperienced actors and by some not very good drama teachers, "You have to take diaphragm lessons. You have to be able to speak from your diaphragm so that you can be heard up in the last row of the theater. You must learn to bring your voice from the diaphragm, push it up, squeeze it out so that it will resound into the audience."

Well, I almost squeezed myself to death trying to be heard in the balcony. I'm serious. I was constipated during half my early performances. My stomach was always in one of those Canadian isometric exercises. I mean it was like a *knot*, I developed such muscles around my diaphragm from *squeezing* everything out of me all the time.

Other widely held attitudes with no real basis in fact were slipped to me as gospel from the actors' bible. For example, if I was playing a tough guy, I was to remember that all tough guys walked tough, talked tough, breathed tough, smelled tough, *spit* tough. That forced me into caricatures you wouldn't believe. To play a tough guy I would go around with my hands ready to strangle somebody, my mouth twisted; I would lower my voice and really be breathing fire, you know what I mean? Well, I looked ridiculous trying to play a tough guy. Not that I *couldn't* play a tough guy—but I was under the impression that in order to be the tough guy, you had to create that tough guy out of external appearances.

When I began to learn what acting and life are all about, I realized that some tough guys look very feminine, some are skinny and not particularly tall and not particularly strong, and some have voices that are kind of tinny. Some of them, if you were to assess them on first impressions, look like priests, others like file clerks or service station attendants or bookworms. I wince when I think back to the times when I was playing tough guys and squeezing my diaphragm. I must have looked something awful up there on the stage. But in the beginning there was no one to tell us that acting at its best was a complex, yet simplified, way of reacting to life's circumstances, and that human beings off the stage spend a large part of their lives doing just that: reacting.

Things might have been otherwise for many talented but inexperienced young actors who have dropped by the wayside if someone had told them that the emotional elements that make up human responses are basically the same in every personality, and have been for millions of years. Why couldn't we have been told that human beings are multitalented in their ability to respond? Our reactions are similar across humanity, yes; but the range of reactions is tremendous. We can respond with anxiety—because we want something to happen, or we don't want something to happen. We can respond with nervousness—physical and emotional—because we're overwhelmed by anxiety over the anticipation of something happening or not happening. We can respond with fear—or a mixture of fear and trepidation and some happiness. A little joy, a lot of joy, other forms of pleasure, or fear of those joys and pleasures. Loneliness, boredom, frustration, self-pity, embarrassment, shame, love, hate, shyness, low self-esteem, exaggeratedly high self-esteem, the fear of rejection and the fear of dying.

In the absence of a guiding light in my early acting, I moved blindly, with misconceptions pointing the way, and as a result I was too many years in coming to understand my craft. But I finally discovered that there's no difference between actor and audience; neither is a stranger to the experiences of life. I'm broadened as an actor the moment I realize that when people sit in a theater and watch me expressing feelings similar to their own, they can tell if I'm really experiencing those emotions or if I'm faking them. Deep down inside, where they've had these same experiences and same responses, they know whether I'm interpreting them in a genuine way or just play-acting. Living consciously involves being genuine; it involves listening and responding to others honestly and openly; it involves being in the moment. This is all equally true of effective acting. Acting isn't a game of "pretend." It's an exercise in being real.

At the point where life and art intersect, John Cassavetes once gave me some advice that has proved invaluable. This was some years ago, when he wanted me to play a particular role. I don't know how, but he sensed reluctance on my part, even though I had said nothing except, "Yes, that would be great. Let's talk about it."

He said, "Let me tell you something." He said, "We're good friends, but never, ever do an artistic favor for a friend. Loan friends money, be there for them in every other way, but don't do them any artistic favors, because you've got to have one area of your life where there's no room for compromise."

That's tough medicine, but I think it holds up absolutely for anyone wishing to create something that will stand the test of time. You simply can't "fake" your way through good work. But even the purest devotion to an art or craft doesn't take place in a vacuum. We work with others, with people often very close to our hearts, so convictions that are firmly held can cost a pretty penny indeed.

I learned this lesson when I came back to live theater in 1960, after having been away from it for ten years. The occasion was *A Raisin in the Sun*, an extraordinary play written by Lorraine Hansberry, produced by Philip Rose, and directed by Lloyd Richards, all of whom were my contemporaries and compatriots.

This experience was for me a confirmation. I had been away from theater but very much engaged in learning about acting; I had been having experiences as an actor in films that altered the way I worked. It had been a very difficult ten years—difficult in that I was determined to develop the ability to recreate close to the bone so that people would feel that what I was doing was natural.

I had just finished *Porgy and Bess* when we went into rehearsal for *A Raisin in the Sun*. Claudia McNeil was to play the mother, I was to play the son, Ruby Dee was to play my wife, Diana Sands was to play my sister, and Glen Furman, all of ten or twelve years old, was to play my son.

We opened in New Haven, then we went to Philadelphia, and then—since the theater that was supposed to be available to us on Broadway wasn't (and wouldn't be for some weeks)— we took the play to Chicago and spent about four weeks polishing.

It was a hugely successful play from the very beginning. There were so many firsts. I had never before seen that kind of focus on black family life. It was a realistic change, a modern change, and it had a tremendous impact.

But it was terribly difficult for me. I can't work on technique alone. I have to work on pure, raw experience, so I had to find a way to get me to raw, organic experience emotionally. I was able to do that for four months, but around about the end of the fourth month it became extremely hard, because I knew the words so well and had to fight against just speaking the lines, just going through the motions.

Broadway theatergoers hadn't been accustomed to seeing this new kind of theater—I mean, theater where they were absolutely grabbed by the power of the piece, and the power of the piece was in its basic human emotions. Just the raw emotions of a mother and a son and a daughter-in-law and a daughter and a grandchild, all caught up in very human tragedies and human difficulties. They were wrenching difficulties between mother and son, son and wife, son and sister, and son and *his* son. The play was a lesson in what humans are really, really all about. People aren't about being black or white. Black and white in the face of *real* issues are mere cosmetics.

I knew for certain that I was meant to be an actor when the curtain came down on opening night in New York. After all the doubts that had accumulated since that serendipitous meeting between myself and that gentleman at the American Negro Theatre, when he threw me out and slammed the door. After all my clumsy efforts at trying to act (like when I read *True Confessions* magazine in my first audition!). After my disastrous opening in *Lysistrata* and all the difficulties I had in remembering the lines. After all the stage fright that had overwhelmed me when I was in acting classes and didn't quite understand what I was about. After all the years of struggling with a craft I couldn't get a grip on. After all those things— that night in 1960 I knew for certain that I had just been formally introduced to my true calling. I had finally learned where the energy was, and how to call on it, how to replenish it, how not to overuse it. That night, *I was an actor.* I had come a long, long way. But I wasn't yet out of the woods. Seven more years would come and go before Rod Steiger and I squared off technique for technique in *In the Heat of the Night.*

I finished a six-month run, but by the time I left the production the actress who played the mother wasn't speaking to me. She hated me. Need I tell you that this is a difficult position to find yourself in as the member of an ensemble of actors?

Claudia McNeil, a fine performer, was in complete dominance over most of the other members of the cast. Naturally enough, she perceived the play as being best when it unfolded from the mother's point of view. *I* perceived the play as being best when it unfolded from the son's point of view, however, and I argued that position. In fact, we argued constantly.

I prevailed, I guess because I was considered the principal player who was responsible for getting the piece mounted. I suppose there might have been some who didn't agree with me but simply acquiesced to my position. But I wasn't just throwing my weight around. I was not, and am not, in the habit of doing that. I genuinely felt that when tragedy fell on the family in *Raisin*, the most devastating effects were visited upon the son, because the mother was such a towering figure.

In my opinion, it was the son who carried the theatrical obligation as the force between the audience and the play. The eyes of those watching were on the son to see if the tragedy would destroy him, would blow him apart beyond recovery. And it was also my opinion that there was no such feeling between the audience and the mother. The audience witnessed the sadness that was visited on her. They saw that her family was in disarray, but they also saw her as a force beyond that kind of vulnerability. If they were to vote, they would say, "Oh, but she's going to be okay."

So where's the drama in the piece?

The drama asks an audience to *care*. This was my argument to the playwright and the director and the producer, all of whom were my friends. If you're going to ask that audience to care, you're going to have to take them to the place where the most damage is possible so they can feel that pain.

If you keep them focused on the mother, they're going to say, "Oh, that's too bad that happened—but listen, that family's going to be okay."

Well, I had learned in my experience as an actor and as a theater participant that wherever there's threatened destruction of a human being, that's where the focus is; and the only existence that was threatened in *Raisin* was the son's. There was simply no guarantee that he would survive. It was fifty-fifty that this boy couldn't do it, wouldn't be able to bounce back. It was highly probable that he wouldn't have the resilience, the guts, the stamina, or the determination. Or, looked at another way, it was possible that he wouldn't be able to experience the catharsis as fully as necessary for him to be reborn. That's what the audience had to see to be fully engaged: the rebirth of this person.

Now, there was no ego in that. I mean, I was a theater person. I had spent most of my early years in theater—not on Broadway necessarily, but I had done many, many off-Broadway shows. I'd seen dozens and dozens of plays, I'd *worked* in dozens of plays, so I felt comfortable in my sense of what drama is made of, both in theatrical terms and in life terms.

So that was my position, and I was fought tooth and nail on it by the director and the writer and the producer. Ruby Dee and I saw more eye to eye than did either of us with the others, so it was my intent, and she concurred, that I would play the drama on opening night the way I believed it *should* be played. That didn't require changing the words, only making a fundamental change in the attitude of the individual.

Now, this gets to the very core of what acting is. How do you shift the emphasis of a play when, as is the case in *A Raisin in the Sun*, there are two characters who are very forceful and quite strong? Here's how: if you see the son's need as not just personal but a need on behalf of his family, then the emotional center shifts, and it becomes a different play.

The action of the play turns on the death of the father, and the fact that the mother receives ten thousand dollars in insurance money because her husband was killed in an accident on the job. The son wants to use the money in the most constructive way he can think of, which is to start a business, to move the family in some structural way up from where they are.

The mother, on the other hand, wants to use the money to buy a house. But the son says to her, in effect, "The money used to buy a house wouldn't affect the family circumstances in that I'd still chauffeur for somebody else, my wife still works as a maid, and you'd still work as a maid. There'd be no shifting of dynamics here. But there could be, with some sweat and tears, there could be some shifting of dynamics if that money were used as down payment for a business that we could all work at. Then in two years or five years, what we'd have done would be substantial enough for us to be thinking about getting a house and, hopefully, then the business would grow and we could have two such businesses or three such businesses in ten years by the time my son is ready for college."

That's his argument, and the mother's argument runs something like, "You want to spend that money to open a liquor store?" She insists, "My husband's memory is not going to be tied in with the selling of liquor. I'm going to use that money to buy a house, to put a roof over our heads."

He says to his mother, "Isn't it better that my father's death advances the family? You have a daughter who's going off to college, hopefully, but where is the money coming from? I have a son who is going to be soon a young man. What are the lessons in this for him? I am a chauffeur. Where are we going to be down the line? Am I going to be a chauffeur at the age of sixty, and is my son going to take over chauffeuring?"

So that's the heart of it. Therefore, the playing of this man has to be such that the audience believes that his need for his family is absolutely elemental, and that this is the last chance, *his* last chance. If he fails now, he'll never be able to gather the steam, gather the courage and the determination to spend himself again in a losing effort. He just won't be able to.

It's this sense of possible destruction that prepares the audience for tragedy when the mother *does* give him the money, after he really fights and struggles for it, and the money is lost. All of it.

The audience is primed to see either total destruction of this man or his resurrection, you follow? But there's no resurrection for the mother, regardless. She gives the money to her son because she finally decides to let him have his shot at being a man, his own man—and then he fucks it up. Well, sad as it might be for her as a mother, there's no great tragedy in that for her as an individual. She loses ten grand that she didn't really have in the first place.

But this young man—he's destroyed. That's what the audience assumes. But in the third act he comes out of the ashes, and that's where the real drama is, because he looks at that boy of his, and he talks to him. In fact, he's talking to the audience *through* the boy; and when he speaks, the audience just goes nuts. I mean, it's so *dramatic*.

Well, that was my position—the position I acted from. The other position, as I said, was held very strongly by the actress who played the mother, as well as by the producer, the director, and the playwright—my friends. When I left the fold to go make movies and they had to replace me, the several men who, over time, took the part had to play it the other way, the mother's way, because the continued success of the play depended on having Claudia McNeil.

Well, the audiences didn't seem to mind one bit. The play continued to work well because it had garnered such recognition by then. And the guys who took over the part were all very fine actors, all extremely fine actors, one of whom was Ruby Dee's husband, Ossie Davis.

So what was the lesson in all this?

I would say that sometimes convictions firmly held can cost more than we're willing to pay. And irrevocable change occurs when we're not up to paying, and irrevocable change occurs when we *are* up to paying. Either way, we have to live with the consequences. If I'm up to paying the price in a certain situation, I walk away from the experience with some kind of self-respect because I took the heat. And if I go the other way, feeling that the cost is too high, then however bright the situation turns out, I feel that something is missing.

For an actor to go onstage every night with the sort of hostile undercurrent we experienced with *A Raisin in the Sun*—it can only be described as being like a bad marriage. I felt that Claudia McNeil wasn't giving me what I needed. She knew where my big moments were, and she knew when to hold back and take the air out—and I lived through that opposition for months.

It was very painful for me to know the effect our disagreement was having on my colleagues. If you're a producer, certainly you're irritated by dissension that threatens to interrupt the life of a hit play. Now, my friend Philip Rose, the producer, disagreed with me completely, and I believe that his disagreement was genuine, because I've known the man all these years, and today he's still one of my closest friends. But at the time, I was leaving his play. He had a play that would run, if he could hold it together and keep Claudia McNeil happy, for years and years. So he wasn't especially sympathetic to my concerns.

The playwright's sympathies were completely against me. She saw the play as weighted toward the mother; that's how she'd *written* it. She was a very intelligent young black woman, and she came from a family of achievers. Her whole family were achievers, especially the women, and she had a certain mindset about women and their potential, especially black women in America. So she wrote a play about a matriarch faced with this dilemma. But in that formulation the son is just a ne'er-do-well. He's a fuckup, not a tragic figure, not a man whose life is on the line. I simply couldn't do it that way, because in my mind the dramatic possibilities were so much greater the other way.

Then, of course, there was the director, Lloyd Richards. Again, a very close friend with whom I had very little quarrel on the question, because his first responsibility was to the work by the playwright. He had gone inside the play with her; she had taken him on an excursion into the inner selves of these characters. So he saw the play as she conceived it, and when he put it together, he put it together that way. He didn't have any conflict with it. But I did—because I had to face an audience, you know?—and I just couldn't face an audience playing it with less than the attitude I thought was necessary for this drama.

Out of town in New Haven I played it their way, but I was looking for answers. I wasn't altogether comfortable. We went on to Philadelphia. Same thing. The play was working fine, but there was something missing. It was working overall, but I wasn't really there. We went to Chicago. Same thing. So Ruby Dee and I started exploring, and in Chicago magic started to happen. Wham! And I started to play differently.

Then we went to New York, and on opening night the energy was at its apex. The director saw it, but he wouldn't characterize the added excitement he sensed as coming from the way I had played the role. The producer saw it too, but he said it was just a great night. The playwright was in the audience, and I went out and helped her up on the stage so that all the world could see this magnificent young woman, this gifted person. She assumed that the incredible night of theater we'd all just experienced was as she wrote it.

Well, I say it played well because there was something special in the conviction I held, and I carried it from Chicago to New York.

There's a special moment in the third act, just before the end. They had put a down payment on a house before they lost the money, but a man comes to tell them that they're not wanted in that neighborhood. My character, the son, has to stand up and talk to this man. He's talking to this man about his family. After a given point in the speech, he says, "This is my mother." Then he says, "This is my sister." And then he says, "This is my wife,—and she is"—pride, pain, and love overpower him and he's not able to get her name out. And by the time he turns to his son, his emotions are more than any words could express. The tears roll down his cheeks and he begins to cry. He gestures to the boy, but the words won't come out, and finally he forces out the words. He says, "This is my son," and the house goes nuts, you hear me?

I know from my own experience that when a guy is just afraid, and he wishes to succeed *because he's afraid of failure,* that's not much of a commitment. But there's another kind of drive to succeed. I think of my father, going from bar to bar selling his cigars, probing my arm because he's worried that I'm not getting enough to eat. Then sitting down to write a letter to his eldest son, telling him that he's no longer able to control and guide his youngest, that he needs help. You find a man like that, with a need to do something that's over and above his own ego-requirement—a need that's for his *family*, as he sees it—and you get every ounce of his energy. When a man says, "This is for my *child*," you get over and above that which he thinks he's capable of.

My father was with me every moment as I performed in *A Raisin in the Sun*. The themes, too, seemed like so many threads from my own life. The days in Nassau and Miami and New York when I seemed to be in such a downward spiral and there was no promise of resurrection. All the risks I took, all the brushes with destruction. I know how much it pained my family, but there was nothing they could do. It was this art form that saved me. Ultimately, by taking even greater risks—by going to New York and then by choosing a life in the theater—I came through. And it wasn't just for myself. It was for Reggie too.

My work reflects that respect for the bloodline. When I commit to a job, I go into a kind of hibernating mode. I start with the script. I read it. And I don't just lie around and skim it, mind you; I read it with no distractions, in a very quiet place. In my mind I go to work, and the words on the page, the descriptions, the words of the characters, the words of *my* character—my mind's eye takes all these and creates visual images. So I look at all of the images and scenes and backgrounds at the same time I'm looking at the needs and the wants and the fears and the hopes and the dreams of the characters, mine included. And during each reading of the script I remember first impressions. By the third or fourth or fifth reading of the script, first impressions have given way to richer and more detailed images, and then I start taking on the words that create these images in my feelings. When there's a contradiction in a speech, behavior, or text that relates to my character I go on a long search trying to find a way to bridge that contradiction by not changing the author's words. Because sometimes the flaw is in the actor not the words.

I look for themes that say something positive and useful about the human condition. I look for that material; I draw all of me into it. When I first read *A Patch of Blue*, what attracted me to it was the attempt to salvage a human life, and the depiction of the amount of energy such an effort can take. But I think that, in an effort like that, life itself is the central force. The energy expended by all the players in that movie was directed to extending ourselves and enlarging ourselves so that we could partake of that preexisting force.

In that film the girl had no sight, so—metaphorically at least—the seat of her soul was elsewhere. Her ears and her fingers were employed in service to her soul. Through those senses, she could preceive dangers of every kind—hear it in people's voices; feel it in the air. She wanted to be a whole person, but she was in a world that didn't give a shit. Then she happened, by chance, to cross paths with a man who knew quite a bit about how little the world did or didn't care about a lot of things, and he took the time to give a little of himself to someone in need. By doing that, he saved her life. It's that simple, *that simple.*

Now, I think the lasting value of the movie was the comment it made, not about me or any of the other characters, but ultimately about humankind. It may sound perfunctory, or simplistic, or even naïve, but I think it's fair and useful to observe that there are wonderful things about our species. My feeling is borne out by the fact that the picture still appears on television periodically, and people are still moved by it. We're talking about something captured on film more than thirty years ago. The life of that girl and the life of this guy are informing people who weren't even born when the film was made.

I was thirty-nine years old when that film was released. Now, at seventy-two, I don't think a month goes by that I don't hear from three or four people about that movie. Either they saw it years ago and remember it as one of the most moving films they've seen, or they've just seen it and love it. "Whatever happened to that girl?" they often ask. Many of these people who talk to me about the film are now thirty-five years old, thirty, twenty-two—and they're seeing it for the first time. And they don't just say, "Oh, I remember that picture, yeah," and go on to something else. They say, "That was with the blind girl. Oh, yes, that's right, and you stopped in the park with her, and you really took care of her. That was really nice. I liked that picture."

I come to *A Patch of Blue* with a fondness and with a sense of satisfaction that I was a part of that piece of work then, that I was knowingly, *knowingly* a part of it over and above the professionalism. I, as well as Guy Green and Pandro Berman and the others, we all embraced it. We all chose to be a part of it because of the value we saw in it.

Freud once said that life is love and work. But if you do *bad* work, it can't provide the meaning in your life that you need from it. I feel most critical of myself when I notice any trace of slovenliness in my work. My work is *me*, and I try my damnedest to take very good care of me, because I'm taking care of more than just the me that one sees. I'm taking care of the me that represents a hell of a lot more than me. I'm taking care of Evelyn, you hear me? And I'm taking care of Reggie.

EIGHT

LEGACIES

BACK IN THE HEYDAY of my acting career, I took a vacation in Acapulco with my agent Marty Baum and some other dear friends. On a gorgeous afternoon, Marty and I left our wives roasting under the tropical sun and went for a swim forty feet offshore. A solitary lifeguard was perched on top of a wooden lookout tower, but he was engrossed in a magazine, not us. Like two carefree adolescents joyfully skinny-dipping in a water hole, we splashed about in the bright blue ocean, clowning and laughing.

Life didn't get any better than this. For a moment there, it was all peace and plenty. We were on top of the world, enjoying the pleasures that, after years of hard work, seemed only our due.

After about fifteen minutes of this blissfulness offshore, we began to breaststroke our way back to the beach. But by now something had changed. When we had first entered the water, we had been surprised to find that the beach didn't *gradually* descend into the sea. Instead, it plummeted straight down a sheer wall of sand, falling quickly from about knee depth to a depth of fourteen feet or so.

Now, as we headed back toward shore, the water temperature was different. The currents were different too. As we came within a few feet of the wall of sand, a turbulence from below started pulling at our legs—pulling *forcefully*. Scared to death, we swam harder, but for all our thrashing we made no progress. Then the ocean rose up beneath us. It wasn't a wave on the surface of the water. It was a raging, thundering swell that lifted off the floor of the sea and slammed itself against the wall of sand, then exploded upward and over onto the beach in a mighty rush of foaming waters. The momentum of that angry wave yanked us free of the undercurrents that were pulling at our legs and flung us violently into the shallows of the beach. Relieved to feel the sand under our feet, we started wading through the receding water on our way to higher ground and safety, up toward the ridge where our wives were sunbathing, paying us no mind.

But then the receding water took hold. With increasing momentum it overpowered us, pulling us back toward the sea. In a panic, we clawed at the sand, trying desperately to plant our feet against the pull of the ocean. But we were outmatched, sucked back to the edge of the wall and pushed fourteen feet down to the bottom. The churning undertow twirled us around like rag dolls in a washing machine. For seven or eight seconds it held us there until another incoming wave, thundering along on the floor of the sea, smashed into the wall of sand, reversed the momentum, and pushed us up again to the surface and onto the beach. Once more we scrambled to our feet, wading and clawing our way upward in another desperate effort to get free of the tide. But again the ocean reversed its momentum. Again we were pushed back down along the wall of sand to the bottom of the sea, back into the turmoil of the undertow.

By now we knew the intervals between waves. The seconds ticked away. We held our breath and prayed that another swell would toss us up again. One more chance, please, God. Then it came, smashing into the wall, pushing us ahead of it and once more onto the beach. We wasted no time checking on each other. It was every man for himself, running, wading, clawing, scrambling with the tide. We got as far up the beach as we could before the moment of truth. We dug in and braced ourselves. We cried and prayed, and I'm sure I called at least once for my mother.

Then the tide reversed, causing billions of grains of sand to swirl around our legs and erode out from under our feet, loosening our grip on life. With every ounce of strength left in us, we tried to hold our ground, but there was no holding against that tide. It had come to take us down for the last time.

We screamed for our wives, their eyes closed against the sun, and we screamed for the lifeguard, still focused on his magazine. They didn't hear us. And then it came again, the sea, pulling us back into itself, and down we went for the third time. And then, amid the violent turning and twisting in that undertow, serenity began to enfold me. "O God," I thought, "has my time really come? Is this sense of well-being here to ease me through that final barrier?"

No answer. Just turmoil. "Lord, I ain't ready to die here," I confessed. "I'm simply not ready. I'm *certainly* not ready to die on the beach in Acapulco." There seemed to be seven or eight seconds between waves. I prayed, "O Lord, don't let the wave be late. If we're forced to breathe down here, it will be all over. Let it come on time; please, Father, don't let it be late. A few seconds off the mark and we'll be done for."

Suddenly the wave arrived, with no time to spare, and it smashed into the wall of sand and jettisoned us up to the surface and onto the beach. I checked to see if Marty had made it up this time. I spotted him ten feet away, half-conscious. The man had started to take in water. He was coughing from having tried to hold his breath beyond endurance, and he was turning blue. Now I had to scream for both of us; Marty no longer had the strength. I screamed and screamed and screamed.

At long last that dummy on top of the tower looked up, saw the situation, and started down the steps. But he was coming down at a rate that said clearly, Oh, shit, why do you guys have to interrupt my reading? As he sauntered over I screamed, yelled, and struggled to hold on. The unrelenting sea paid no heed. Marty Baum and I were swallowed up once more. But this time at least I knew that somebody was coming. I had to hang on.

I was tossed forward and backward and twirled and spun, but I hung on and waited. It was like an underwater sandstorm down there. I could only hold my breath and close my eyes and hope. With consciousness fixed on my last view of the life-guard strolling in our direction, I managed to hang on until the next wave brought me up. I was too weak to do anything more than look over toward the lifeguard, who was standing in the water waiting for Marty. When Marty came up this last time, the guard grabbed him and pulled against the tide. Mir-aculously, he was able to drag Marty up on the beach to safety.

In the meantime, I was dragged down once again. I had fought all I could. I found myself crossing over to a place where struggle was no longer necessary; all I could do was relax. I was pretty sure that if I got tossed up again, and if that lifeguard was there, I would be okay. Otherwise, I didn't think there was anything I could do about it.

My children were on my mind each time I came up and each time I went back down. I worried about how they would get their education, how they would manage. Would their mother be able to get a job and continue to make a home for them? How would my family react back in Nassau when they heard that I'd drowned? All this was going through my mind as I held my breath. And while you may not be able to visualize this, take my word for it—I was turning blue.

One more time I was tossed up on the beach, and I opened my eyes to see a pair of legs in the sand. The lifeguard grabbed me and I grabbed him. He hung on to me for dear life, and after the water receded, he dragged me up and dropped me by

Marty, who by now was coughing and choking. We lay there side by side like two beached mackerels. Our wives came dashing over, and soon a doctor arrived on the scene and declared us to be okay.

We hadn't been okay twenty minutes before we began laughing and telling jokes about it all. But I guarantee you there was no sacrilege in our laughter. Tears we had shed aplenty, and genuine prayers for mercy had filled our hearts while nature held our fragile existence in the balance for an absolutely critical few minutes. A reprieve had been granted, and we knew it.

Close calls like this—"Nearer, my God, to thee" moments—inevitably make us stop and take stock. Almost invariably, the calibrations by which we measure ourselves move inward. It often takes a near-death experience like ours to make us realize how simple life is, how few the essentials really are. We love; we work; we raise our families. Those are the areas of significance in our individual lives. And love and work and family are the legacy we leave behind when our little moment in the sun is gone.

We never had a pot to piss in when I was small, but my parents left me great riches in the form of a childhood that's traveled with me down every path I've taken. Ironically, though, there may be more to the legacy of Evelyn and Reggie Poitier than love and warmth and the solid ground beneath my feet.

When my father died, he made me the executor of his estate, and in sorting out his affairs, I went back to the time when it first became possible for blacks to own land in the Bahamas,

which was 1858. Because of the vestiges of colonial possession, the ownership of land in these islands has always been
fraught with mystery, but back a century and a half there were
several ways in which black families could obtain land.

In some cases, slaveowning families would simply bequeath
land to their former chattel. In other cases, as the plantation system began to falter, families would abandon land and sail back
to England or the Carolinas, opening up their property to a
kind of "squatter's rights." And finally, after 1858, once black
people were allowed to own land, they could, over time, simply buy it out of the few shillings a month they might earn.

My father, in his years on Cat Island, became caretaker for a
certain portion of land. He was in charge of land on behalf of
absentee landlords, who left him there to look after the land. He
had a right to farm, and to take care of the paths that had to be
cut with machetes, but caretakers too could work the land as
much as they wished for their own needs. If, by chance, one of
the owners lived on the land or visited there, then the caretaker
had to supply the casabas and the beans and the peas and whatever for the landowner as well.

There's a law in the Bahamas that states that if you can prove
you were for a substantial amount of time once the caretaker of
land now abandoned and unused by absent, former slaveowner
families, you can, under certain provisions, claim rights to that
land. That law is currently at play where my family is concerned, and ownership of several pieces of land is being adjudi-
cated on the basis of my father's verifiable service as caretaker
and overseer. My dad also owned other land there outright. My

grandfather March owned land as well, and my grandfather's father had owned land, having purchased it over time with earnings. In addition, my uncle David, who traded goods and ran a sort of grocery store, had acquired land through the barter system, meaning that, at times, he had traded groceries for land. When he died, this land went to my father.

Of course, the recordkeeping on Cat Island was problematic at best during the time in question. In the early days the colonials were very clever, and hardly any of the slaves could read very well. That combination spelled trouble for the rights of the blacks. If a white family had left certain property rights or a patch of land to a slave, the slave had only one place to go to prove that: to the records that were kept by the church (because the government kept no records for black people). So after it became known that slavery had ended and black people could own property *if they had the proper records*, whenever a black person wanted to assert rights to a piece of property, he had to say, "Well, in his will my master left me this piece of land here, and here's where he marked it off. He marked it off here and here and here, and I have this piece of paper that shows . . ."

The black person would then have to go to a white person, who would put the claim in writing, and the former slave would have to put an X to the document. That would authenticate the claim in favor of the former slave. Well, an awful lot of that land was confiscated through the misuse of this trust, you know what I'm saying? Because the white person who was the scribe would just say, "This land was left to so and so, and it is to be so and so and so and so, and I, so and so, declare that this is true." Well, an unscrupulous person could put in that phrase anything he wanted to put in it, because who's to say otherwise?

But despite all such chicanery in the past, and despite all the hardships and disappointments, if my family can substantiate our claim—and I believe we will—then it appears that Reggie Poitier will have left to his heirs a substantial portion of beach-front property on an unspoiled Caribbean island, an estate of not inconsiderable value.

The irony of the situation pleases me. It will be a marvelous vindication for my father if the land is declared his, and a testa-ment to the importance of the bloodline, the primal connection, and to holding on for the long haul, through all the changes from one generation to the next.

WHEN I WENT BACK to the Bahamas after my time of ashes in New York, despite the joy I experienced on seeing my parents again after eight years, I had changed irrevocably. I stayed in a hotel. I didn't wish to use the outhouse with its brown-paper-bag or green-leaf toilet paper. I didn't want to have to carry water a quarter mile to have a wash-up. I didn't want to have to build a fire to heat the water before I could take a bath. I wanted to turn a faucet and have limitless hot water. I wanted to flip a switch and have light. After eight years of struggle I was able to return to my father's house, but in certain ways I was never able to go back home.

But looked at another way, it may be that I'm always "at home." Thanks to the more fundamental legacy my parents gave me, I'm always at home because I'm the same person no matter where I am. I'm the same person at some Hollywood dinner that I was when I was being hassled by the cops in Miami or sleeping in a pay toilet in New York. It's that consistent definition of self, I'm sure, that allowed me to get through the tough times, when others were more than happy to try to define me according to their own prejudices.

For some people this kind of situation would pose a wrenching conflict. You come from one place and you find yourself in another place. Which one represents who you really are? Oddly, for me, the answer is very simple. I've lived a lot of places, but in every place I've lived, what's basic and fundamental in me has remained the same. The same guiding principles were operative on 5th Avenue as in Harlem; the same on 68th Street on the West Side as when I left Cat Island.

Still, there's something called "poverty syndrome." You can't have been subject to poverty at one time and ever live free of it again. It hunkers down in your head and latches on to your very being. It can be subdued; it can be varnished over; it can even in some cases be neutralized. But boy, external circumstances can bring it right out of its dormant state again.

After all these years I'm still very careful how I spend money, *very* careful, because there's a fear somewhere deep down inside myself—I don't let it rise to the surface, but I know where it's resting—that one day I'll wake up and everything will all be gone! I'll be back to the poverty level, where just surviving from morning to night is a real challenge. We live in the most litigious society in the world, and we all know that all kinds of unexpected things can happen.

I never spend with abandon or disregard for what money represents. And just what is that? Well, what it represents isn't what I *am*, though I worked hard and I earned this money, and it's mine. No, what it represents is good fortune, because I'm a lucky son of a gun. Most people aren't that fortunate, materially speaking. So first of all, I need to accept and be joyous about the fact that I've been so lucky. And then, since I *have* been so lucky (and others haven't), I have to remember the corollary: with luck come some responsibilities—one of which is "Don't piss on it."

We live in a world in which all things are relative. Being rich means one thing for someone of my background and experience, and it has quite a different meaning for someone else. Not that a person's definition of wealth necessarily remains static. As circumstances change, so does that definition.

With the sensibilities of a kid off a primitive island in the Caribbean, I felt rich each time I got paid *anything* during those early years. I can remember a time when, if I could have been guaranteed the income of fifty bucks a week for the rest of my life, I would have perceived myself as not just rich but *super-rich*. Then came a time when I thought that the accumulation of a hundred thousand dollars would be an overwhelming experience; and to have that and then *also* maybe have a job paying fifty bucks a week—I mean, what else could someone wish for? But now, much later in life, my perceptions are different.

I have friends who are billionaires, and I have friends who are struggling to pay four hundred dollars in rent every thirty days—and I can see it all from a much broader perspective.

By the standards of Cat Island, even the standards of Nassau, I'm wildly rich today, but the really profound changes I've experienced are much more subtle. As your life unfolds and you become better off, you become accustomed to a room in a motel that's clean and comfortable, and there's this wonderfully clean bathroom, and there's a television set and a telephone. That, at one stage in your life, is heaven right there. At another stage heaven becomes the Plaza Hotel, a two-bedroom suite, where the bathroom is all marble, and there are dressing gowns in the closet. After a while, if you reach that level and stay there for a bit, that degree of luxury, too, becomes pedestrian. But the one constant is that you can't go back. Well, you might be able to manage if you were *forced* to, but you won't ever *elect* to go back.

My father, in his days, was never so fortunate in a material way. Eventually, poverty simply wore him down—but I will say, to his credit, that it took seventy-seven hard years. Despite all the strength and forbearance that kept him going through every other form of hardship, arthritic crippling was at last too much for him, and he simply chose to let go. He called in a young lawyer one day, ostensibly to talk about land claims, and while they were at it he dictated a simple two-page will. Then, beginning the next day, he refused to eat. Not blatantly, so as to call attention to himself. But subtly. He received the meals my mother brought to him on the porch; then, as she turned away to resume her chores, he gave the food to the neighborhood's scavenger dogs. It was five days before my mother got wise to what he was doing, but by then the doctors at Princess Margaret Hospital couldn't save him. Especially since he was so determined that he had lived enough.

Let me assure you, my father was a man of will and determination. I remember one time when we were living in Nassau. My sister Teddy, a grown woman at this point, was having trouble with the men in her life and wanted to come home. She was separated from her husband and had been living with a wild fellow named Blood, who was trouble. My father told her, "Okay, you can come home for a while. But once you're home, you don't belong to him—you become a part of our family once again. We're going to put the protection of this family around you. Therefore, you have a responsibility to this family not to see him without my permission. You're not to go back to his house, agreed?"

Well, she agreed to those terms, but before long she was seeing Blood again, and then my father found out.

"Is it true what I heard?" he asked her. When she just hung her head without answering, he said to her, "Go out there to that tamarind tree and bring me a switch."

I knew from personal experience that the tamarind switch was the worst thing to get a whipping with because it had thornlike knots and jagged edges. But he took it, and even though Teddy was a woman maybe twenty-four years old, with two children of her own, he beat the daylights out of her. As he did he said to her, "If I tell you that this house is my home, and if I tell you that under this roof you have to do what I tell you—you have to respect this house and respect me—you listen and you do it. Under my roof you never get so old or so big that you're outside the jurisdiction of my parenting."

Reggie Poitier knew what his legacy would be. He knew and believed in the importance of his role as a father, and he knew that it extended well beyond his capacity as a breadwinner. He believed in the responsibility and the dignity of his task as a bearer of standards, and as an *enforcer* of standards, and he wouldn't let his relative position in the economic hierarchy of a crazy tourist economy in any way belittle that *tribal* role. God knows economic forces had done everything they could to bend him. He had been driven off the land as a tomato farmer, reduced to selling cigars here and there in Nassau watering holes, but when discipline was needed, he still had the wherewithal to say, "Go get me the tamarind switch."

The fact is you can't do that kind of parenting if your values aren't clear to you in terms of your own life. You can't be passing on to your kids a strong foundation if you don't have one yourself—because whatever foundation you do or don't have, that's what you're going to pass on. And when we pass on something that doesn't serve our children, we have to be responsible for that.

In my generation we did a lot of pleasure-chasing—we, the generation responsible for today's twenty-year-olds and thirty-year-olds and forty-year-olds. Before they came into our lives, we were on a pleasure binge, and the need for immediate gratification passed through us to our children.

When I got out of the Army in 1944, the guys who were being discharged with me were mostly between the ages of eighteen and thirty. We came home to a country that was in great shape in terms of industrial capacity. As the victors, we decided to spread that good fortune around, and we did all kinds of wonderful things—but it wasn't out of selfless idealism, let me assure you. Take the Marshall Plan, which we implemented at that time. It rebuilt Europe, yes, but it also enabled those war-ruined countries to buy from us. The incredible, explosive economic prosperity that resulted just went wild. It was during that period that the pleasure principle started feeding on itself.

One generation later it was the sixties, and those twenty-eight-year-old guys from World War II were *forty*-eight. They had kids twenty years old, kids who had been so indulged for two decades that it caused a huge, first-time-in-history distortion in the curve of values. And, boy, did that curve bend and bend and bend.

These postwar parents thought they were in nirvana if they had a color TV and two cars and could buy a Winnebago and a house at the lake. But the children they had raised on that pleasure principle of material goods were by then bored to death. They had overdosed on all that *stuff*. So that was the generation who decided, "Hey, guess where the *real* action is? Forget the Winnebago. Give me sex, drugs, and rock 'n' roll." Incredible mind-blowing experiences, head-banging, screw-your-brains-out experiences in service to immediate and transitory pleasures.

But the one kind of gratification is simply an outgrowth of the other, a more extreme form of the same hedonism, the same need to indulge and consume. Some of those same sixties kids are now themselves forty-eight. Whatever genuine idealism they carried through those love-in days got swept up in the great yuppie gold rush of the eighties and the stock market nirvana of the nineties—and I'm afraid we are still miles away from the higher ground we seek.

For most of human history, most people were only slightly above the starvation level. (In many countries, most people *still* are.) Families needed every one of their six or nine kids to toe the line. Otherwise, as everyone knew at every moment, the whole family wouldn't make it. The new postwar prosperity meant that you could laugh at the old duffers who had grown up in the Great Depression and kept crying caution. The great god Necessity was turned aside by, "Well, shit. Who cares? Everyone we know is prosperous, everything's prosperous, and I'm bored."

When my mother sent me for water, which had to be drawn a long way from the house, it was because she needed to cook with it and to wash our pots with it. If I had said, "Nah, I don't feel like it," I know what the result would have been. If my *mother* hadn't kicked my ass, my *brother* would have kicked my ass. My brother would have said, "Are you crazy? Grab that pot over there and get that water!" That was the ritual. That was the way it worked.

I hope that doesn't put me in the category of old duffers. I don't mean to be like some old guy from the olden days who says, "I walked thirty miles to school every morning, so you kids should too." That's a statement born of envy and resentment. What I'm saying is something quite different. What I'm saying is that by having very little, I had it *good*. Children need a sense of pulling their own weight, of contributing to the family in some way, and some sense of the family's interdependence. They take pride in knowing that they're contributing. They learn responsibility and discipline through meaningful work. The values developed within a family that operates on those principles then extend to the society at large. By not being quite so indulged and "protected" from reality by overflowing abundance, children see the bonds that connect them to others.

Dirt poor and wearing a gunnysack for pants, I inherited such a legacy, and I pity the kids today who are being raised in such a way that they'll be hard-pressed to enjoy the simple things, to endure the long commitments, and to find true meaning in their lives.

Poverty didn't kill my soul. Poverty can destroy a person, yes, but I've seen prosperity kill many a soul as well. After so much ease and comfort and mindless consumption of commodities, how do we even know that anything resembling a soul is there anymore? One way is to look to people who are still making enduring commitments. That's where heroes like Nelson Mandela come in. That man broke rocks for thirteen years! You don't go to prison for twenty-seven years for your beliefs if what you believe in is unbridled pleasure. To make that kind of sacrifice, you have to believe that there's something more to it all than "he who dies with the most toys wins." But who among us today is going to take that kind of stand? Who among us believes that strongly in any ideal or ideology?

The laws of economics don't promote idealism or higher consciousness. The logic of profit and loss in a market-driven culture reduces the grandeur of the human species down to one role, that of "consumers." And all along, the pleasure principle is saying, "I have products I can sell you to take care of all that. You can get it online. Come, come. I have even more thrills to show you."

We're not nearly as strong as our mothers and fathers were. I mean, to endure—to just simply stand up under the strain for a lifetime of what someone like my mother had to put up with. But she endured because she found comfort in her *commitments*. She stoked the fire and she tended the farm and she washed the clothes and she baked the bread, but she found a *satisfaction* in that. The physical demands of that load would have been enough to smother and overwhelm many people, but they didn't her, because she wasn't infected by the pleasure principle. She didn't flick a switch and have the lights go on and electrical power rush to her command to wash the clothes, to heat the oven. She couldn't just turn on the water and let it run out of a tap. What she had instead—commitment—was even better.

What a life for a woman: getting up before the sun and working until darkness fell, washing her dishes and scrubbing out her pots by candlelight—and that's if she was lucky enough (or, to use the proper word, *rich* enough) to own a candle. Even the small convenience of a *candle* was a gift. You can't imagine what a gift that was in my mother's time. If she had half a dozen candles in the house, she would light only one per night and let it burn maybe just so much and then put it out. She would tend to it with such care—savor it, conserve it.

Now the kids of her children and her grandchildren— they're so accustomed to convenience that they can't find any pleasure in such small delight.

A little hardship is a good thing, then. But how much? It's a difficult trade-off—especially when we're talking about our children.

As I've mentioned, a large part of my father's legacy is the lesson he taught his sons. He brought us together and said, "The measure of a man is how well he provides for his children."

That teaching weighed heavily on me when my first wife and I separated. That breakup was a long, painful, scarring period for all concerned. Juanita, my wife, had no interest in dismantling the family. She knew that there was great dissatisfaction on my part, but she was a good Catholic girl, and with that background you stay the course, you take the good with the bad. You accept inconvenience and painful readjustments, and sometimes you just absorb the painful elements in the marriage that can't be excised.

Of course, too, I was in love with another woman, and the guilt of that was something that eleven years of psychotherapy couldn't "cure." There was a time when the pain was so intense that I cast blame in all directions. "My wife doesn't understand me enough," I would say in clichéd fashion. And then I would say that the "other woman" had her own agenda.

It was all a pretty miserable situation. Especially knowing that my mother and my father had done so much better. My brothers Reginald and Cedric had done so much better. And then came Sidney, who simply wasn't measuring up. In fact, I was *giving* up.

All I knew was that I had to get to the other side. And in the midst of all this pain, there were my kids. I had to tell them that it wasn't their mother's fault, it wasn't the "other woman's" fault, it was *my* fault.

My good friend Harry Belafonte had gone through the heartache of a divorce a few years ahead of me. Harry saw me in great pain, and I asked him if he knew someone I could talk to. He recommended a psychiatrist, and then he said to me, from his own experience, "Always be there for your children, no matter what. If they're supposed to come visit you and they don't want to, they've *got* to come," he said. "If they don't want to talk to you, they don't have to talk to you; but they have to be there. You can put the food on the table, but they don't have to eat. They can spend the whole weekend in their rooms, but they're going to know that you cared enough to have them with you. And you take them back on Sunday evening, and you don't get them again till two weekends later, or whatever the situation is."

He spoke with the fervor of a preacher by this point. "And you pick them up again the next time, faithfully, and you bring them to your place. If they want to go to a movie, you drop them off and then go back and pick them up, and then you take them home and you help them to get ready for bed and you do for them whatever they need. And if they don't say one word to you for the whole weekend, you just live with it. When the time comes for them to return to their mom, you get together and you help them get dressed and packed, and you take them back home."

Well, it was some of the best advice I was ever given. It echoed my father's teaching, because I knew that when Reggie talked about providing, he wasn't talking just about material things. I got the same encouragement from my psychoanalyst, with whom I would sit down four or five times a week to face my guilt. And my guilt would stare back at me with no expression. Did it change me? Yes. Did it make me a better person? I don't know. As self-serving as it may sound, it certainly made me a better father.

I found it in myself to face up to the conflicts I had created. I didn't walk away from my children. I took an apartment in New York, but every day I went back up to the suburbs where they lived to be there when they got home from school or when they gathered for their dinner. Years later, they began, in their own words, to let me know that it was good for them to know that I was there for them. And I *was* there for them, even when I traveled far from home for work. Wherever I went in the world, I would leave in their care a phone number. And I now have one hell of a relationship with my children.

But it wasn't always so. There were rough passages, to be sure. In my experience with my kids, I would come to a point where the silence would commingle with my guilt, and then I would have to talk. And yet, as I discovered one day with my older children, the more I talked, the more they pulled back.

"Oh, come on, tell me about it. You must be having trouble in school. You must be having trouble with . . ."—name your conundrum.

Their silent response was, "Go away. Get out of my face."

But when I was just present and available and waited for it to happen, the good stuff could start with the most innocuous question.

"How far is it now?"

"Oh, it's not too far."

"Well, what are we going to do when we get there?"

They would begin to wonder about something, and somehow they would open up a little bit, you know? It's really crazy.

My daughter Sydney came home from school one day and sat at the table writing. I said, "What are you doing there? What are you writing?"

She said with great earnestness, "I'm going to write a no-vel." She said, a "no-vel I'm going to write," and I said, "Oh, that's wonderful."

"I'm going to write a no-vel, and I'm working on it now," she repeated.

And like a fool I got it in my head to encourage her. But parents don't know how much weight a simple word can carry. I started encouraging her, and she started pulling back, and within a year she had given up the whole idea. The last thing in the world she wanted to do was write a "no-vel."

With my daughter Beverly, communication was sometimes even harder. She was the oldest, only thirteen or so when Juanita and I separated. The daughter of an outsider and a maverick, she hungered for the insider's state of being, yet I was tearing her world apart.

Once she said to me, "Why do I have to do well in school?"

I said, "Because it's essential to your adult life."

And she said, "Well, I don't want to be a standout. I don't want to be better than anybody else. Why do I have to be better?"

"A good education is a necessity for whatever lifestyle you decide to create for yourself," I replied.

"Well, why can't I be like everybody else? I'd like to be like my friends. *I don't want to be different!*" she screamed, hardening her protest against the list of unpleasant circumstances threatening her sense of safety. Even before the unraveling of her parents' marriage, the social status that my success had brought to the family had begun to be a difficult issue for her with friends at school. She didn't want the responsibility of having to negotiate a compromise between friends, self, and family for fear of forcing all her troubles into open view. For her, being looked upon as different, as not belonging, would be disastrous. She feared being an awkward, self-conscious misfit among regulars, an outsider where she had always found harmony and comfort.

Mainstream society, meanwhile, was sending her negative signals loaded with racial and class overtones, causing her to question her identity and her worth. She, and many like her, faced a worldview so pervasive, so subtly demeaning, so blithely insensitive that even those who were able to evade it would forever carry scars of one kind or another. A few hid their scars in shame; others wore them as merit badges (or so it's hoped).

The net effect on Beverly of my leaving her mother was huge. She stopped speaking to me for two years, dropped out of school, got married at too early an age, and moved to Africa.

One could more than double the number of disappointments and regrets I would be reasonably expected to haul around under the circumstances. The truth of the matter is Beverly's reluctance to finish her education had the most disastrous effect on me. Next to that was the silent treatment she laid on me during the two years of estrangement. While I was always pressing to reestablish and maintain a relationship, she was pressing to have it minimized to a punishing extent. (Alas! Parents, too, must be brought to judgment for their sins.)

By the time she was in her mid-twenties we had made a few encouraging steps toward reconciliation and were doing rather well, as a matter of fact, given the circumstances. Then one day my phone rang. It was Beverly. She said to me, "I looked for a job for months. The only one I found for which I had matching skills was making sandwiches in a delicatessen. I've now been at that job for two weeks. I'm a grown, married lady with two children, and my husband's job doesn't cover the nut. I've had to reexamine my whole life. The reason I'm calling is this: I wondered if you would be willing to give me a little financial help to go back to school?" I said, "Of course." She went back to school, obtained a degree from Southern Methodist University, and is today a writer making a living at her craft.

Looking back on how it must have been for her, I've come to the realization that being an insider among friends must have seemed like a heaven-sent guarantee of comfort and support at what was, for her, the most critical of times. When she was terrified, at thirteen or fourteen years of age, that her family was about to be dismantled by her wayward father—precisely when other pillars underneath her life were showing signs of disintegration—she turned away from me and let her instincts for survival lead her toward the familiar. Comfort and support embraced her, delaying for a time those hard, lonely, personal, but necessary survival struggles through which she would, one day, arrive at being her own person.

———

WHEN I WAS a boy there was a schoolhouse, and it was one room. Sometimes we went and sometimes we didn't, because we were in the fields most of the time.

I got to Nassau at ten and a half, and I quit school at twelve, so what I picked up between Cat Island and Nassau was just enough to read the basics.

But I had a great teacher in Nassau. His name was Mr. Fox, William Fox. We called him Bill, Mr. Bill Fox, and he was magical. I learned more from him than virtually anyone. I drew heavily on him as a model for my character in *To Sir, with Love*.

That was a film that touched many lives. It told of a teacher in a rough-and-tumble section of London, a teacher who stepped into a situation where there was depravity, where there was lack of opportunity, where there was lack of stability, where there was lack of family cohesion, and where there were too many other anxieties and frustrations for kids to be able to learn; and that teacher showed his students other, more meaningful, values and suggested what those values could mean in their lives.

He taught manners to kids who hadn't understood what manners were. In their distorted view, they had considered *good* manners hoity-toity, an affected way of being for people who walked around with their noses in the air. But this teacher taught them otherwise. He also taught about self-respect, dignity, integrity, and honesty, using their own lives as examples.

By the end of the film he had transformed his class into a group of interesting people, most of whom were thinking about going further in education, most of whom were feeling much, much better about themselves and were willing to give each other the benefit of the doubt, who were able to offer respect and to receive respect quite openly. He did all this for them, but he also showed them that they were still the same people that they had been—only better. You don't have to become something you're not to be better than you were.

He also taught them integrity, largely by *showing* them integrity. He offered himself as a friend, and until they were able to understand the offer and accept it, he endured an awful lot. He was driven to anger. He was humiliated. He was threatened with bodily harm. He was dismissed and persecuted.

In the end, though, he succeeded in helping his students to see themselves in this new life as valuable, useful human beings with impressive potential. Just as this transformation came about, a new opportunity opened up for him. He had been applying for engineering jobs throughout the year—in fact, engineering, not teaching, was really his field—and finally a job opened up for him. By now, though, he had developed such a connection to these troubled kids, and to this idea of helping them and transmitting these values, that he decided to stay on. He said no to the dream he had hoped for and stayed to help the next class of disadvantaged students.

I see that decision as showing great courage and great integrity—the kind of courage and integrity that my father had, and that enabled him to say, in effect, "This house may be a shack with no toilet, but in my house these are the rules." The greatest part of that legacy from my father is the knowledge that in discipline and commitment lies hope.

It takes great courage for anyone to raise children properly, and I'm full of respect for those who do it well. When I arrived in Miami at the age of fifteen, my brother Cyril was holding down three jobs to support his family. The man used to get up at four o'clock in the morning and didn't get home until ten o'clock at night. That wasn't for a *season*; that was *all the time*. My brother wasn't an educated person. His primary job was at the airport, where he was a porter; and my sister-in-law was a nurse's aide. He was making maybe fifty dollars a week, and she was probably making thirty-five. So that's eighty-five dollars for two people, black, in Miami, Florida, in

1942. Eighty-five dollars a week. And guess what they did? They put nine kids through college and they bought a house. On eighty-five dollars a week! And it was a nice house. It had electricity. It had two toilets, one and a half baths. It had a kitchen. It had a backyard.

They could do it because they had made a commitment to each other, to those children, and to a certain set of values, and they stayed the course. I admire them tremendously for what they were and what they did.

But can we expect others to do the same thing? Despite all the hardships my brother and sister-in-law endured, and all the racial indignities of Florida at the time, they still had a community and a culture that sustained their hope for something better in days to come—if not for themselves, then for their kids. But what of the poorly skilled and not well educated workers of today? What of the one-fifth of the American public for whom the problem isn't abundance and instant gratification but *no* gratification, and consequently no hope?

Could we expect a young man and a young woman coming of age today to reasonably make the kind of commitment my brother and his wife made? What's the earning power in today's dollars of a man such as my brother who must work with his hands? What are his prospects? And where today is the stable community that would sustain such a couple, where one can be both poor and dignified and raise one's children with decency and hope?

Does our society support that kind of courageous commitment? If the answer is education, does our society adequately provide that tool of self-improvement to the less well off? Between the American mythology of "Pull yourself up by your bootstraps" and the orthodoxy of entitlements, where's the enduring commitment for the long haul, the consistent vision of how to weave the less fortunate into a decent and humane society?

I must ask myself what I've done to support that vision of the future. I know that one can never do enough. "To whom much is given, much is required" the Bible says, and I give money to this and to that and lend my name to certain causes. But where I've invested most in the future of this planet—unreservedly, and from the deep heart's core—is through the lives of six talented and intelligent young women, truly beautiful human beings, whom I burst with pride to call my daughters.

NINE

STARGAZING

ON CAT ISLAND, when I was six or seven, I walked the beaches constantly because they weren't that far from my house. One of the things I always heard on those walks, mixed with the chirping and singing of birds, was the sound of an insect we called a singer (because its screeches sounded like a song). These musical insects were fairly common on the island. You could walk for miles and miles inland or on the beach, and you would hear only the birds and the singers, because there are so few people—just the birds and the singer insects. I remember often walking alone along the beach, listening to the singer insects and searching the nearby coral reefs for stingrays—those great big wonderful, beautiful creatures, so wide it seems as if they have wings.

One day, doing that, I looked upward toward the sky—it was a bright, clear, sunny day—and I saw what looked like something falling into the ocean. I kept looking and there were *more* somethings—and these things kept falling. It looked like a series of objects, and they seemed round, and clear, and quite large, and quite far away. As I followed them down, they landed in the ocean, one by one. Well, after some months, this became a ritual. Whenever I was walking on the beach, I would just look up, and sure as hell there would be these things falling into the ocean. I thought, of course, that they were coming out of the sky, inexplicably, and I wondered what part of the sky they were coming out of and why they were falling into the sea.

When we left Cat Island and went to Nassau, I was no longer near the water all that much, you know? I mean, we were *near* the water in Nassau, but on Cat Island I had gotten up in the morning and *there was the water*. In Nassau things were different, *life* was different, and I had friends and lots of people. I didn't have time for that kind of contemplative thing, strolling on a beach and looking up at a blue sky and seeing objects fall.

Anyway, it would be years before I realized what those things were. I later discovered that what appeared to be objects falling into the sea were really spots in a film over my eyeballs. When I look against a blue sky now, I know that as the film rolls down, any spots in the film—little cells—look as if they're far away and falling as they come across my cornea into the pupil.

But by the time I learned this, I had already learned other things. I somehow had been introduced to the stars, though I hadn't heard the word *galaxy* yet. I hadn't heard the word *cosmos* yet. I hadn't even heard the word *astronomy* yet. Still, I had the sense that there was something out there.

When I learned to read fairly well, I started coming across these words frequently, and every time I came upon something about the stars, I would read it. Much of it, of course, was incomprehensible to me, because I didn't understand the scientific terminology. Somehow, though, I stumbled on the information that a star is a sun, and that there are lots and lots of suns, and that the star we see at night isn't *just* a star, and that the sun we see in the daytime isn't *just* a sun, but that both are one and the same. Well, it took me a while to figure that one out. But the fascination grew—the fascination that had started because of the film rolling over my cornea, creating the impression of crystalline globes falling into the sea.

Years later I had the privilege of getting to know Carl Sagan, even being a guest on his television show. We met and we became kind of friendly, and I saw him at the homes of other people after we had met, and he invited me to the Jet Propulsion Lab in Pasadena.

One evening we had dinner at the home of the director of the lab, and from there we went to the facility. Because they were about to begin receiving the first data from the probe around Neptune, there was a large collection of guests, journalists, and scientists, all gathered in this fabulous room. As the information began to come in, it was processed and then put up on a big screen, and then this chap who was the head of things, he would describe it to the press and to the invited guests, and then Carl would make comments.

Despite his background as a serious scientist, despite all the physics and math he knew, Sagan still had the great capacity to wonder. He was mesmerized by the Saturn discoveries, just as you would have been, or just as I was as a little boy on the beach looking up at the stars. He maintained that sense of wonder throughout his life.

For a long while after he became ill he was still able to move about, he was still on his feet, and they were working and struggling to reverse his illness. Then the time came when they knew that they weren't going to be able to. He went on *Nightline*, I remember, and he talked about his work and, of course, his physical condition. And a question came up about illness and hope. It was phrased as delicately as possible, but the gist of it was, "What are the thoughts of a dying man, and what exactly comes to mind in terms of religion and the afterlife?"

Carl was a scientist to the end (not that there aren't scientists who believe in God). He let it be known that his faith was firmly in science, that he believed science would eventually explain much, much more than we know now, and that those forthcoming technical details would be the only answers we're ever going to have. In other words, he wasn't looking for a hedge in his time of need. He wasn't covering his bets.

Well, I'm no scientist, and certainly I don't have Carl Sagan's technical understanding of the universe and our position within it. I simply believe that there's a very organic, immeasurable consciousness of which we're a part. I believe that this consciousness is a force so powerful that I'm incapable of comprehending its power through the puny instrument of my human mind. And yet I believe that this consciousness is so unimaginably calibrated in its sensitivity that not one leaf falls in the deepest of forests on the darkest of nights unnoticed.

Now, given the immensity of this immeasurable power that I'm talking about, and given its pervasiveness through the universe (extending from distant galaxies to the tip of my nose), I choose not to engage in what I consider to be the useless effort of giving it a name, and by naming it, suggesting that I in any way understand it, though I'm enriched by the language and imagery of both traditional Christianity and old island culture. Many of my fellow human beings *do* give it a name, and *do* purport to understand it in a more precise way than I would ever attempt. I just give it respect, and I think of it as living in me as well as everywhere else.

The grand consciousness I perceive allows me great breadth and scope of choices, none of which are correct or incorrect except on the basis of my own perception. This means that the responsibility for me rests with me.

I have obligations to be in service to this me, to shape it, to encourage its growth, to nurture it toward becoming a better and better me day by day, to be conversant with all its good qualities, such as they are, and to be aware of all its bad qualities, such as they are. When the living space between the two sets of qualities becomes so uncomfortable that choices have to be made, I try to come down on the side of what I feel is right.

I'll say that I believe in God, if you press me to the wall, but then I'm going to come right back at you and give you the above definition of God. You follow? And that's the only definition of God that I'll defend, because I don't think it's possible for me to embrace any other.

I have a kind of respect—a *worshipful* attitude, even—for nature and the natural order and the cosmos and the seasons. I know it's no accident that ancient people celebrated the solstice and the equinox. There's something very powerful that happens, especially in the colder climates of the north, when instead of being a minute shorter every day, daylight lasts a minute longer. You feel it in your bones. You know it as you might know the presence of God. We're halfway there! We may survive this winter after all!

I don't believe in a Moses laying down the law; I simply believe that there are natural harmonies, and that some things work better than others—and it so happens that most of those things that work better than others align pretty well with the Judeo-Christian ethics that most people in this country define as morality. They work better, within the system of life on this planet. They don't violate the natural order.

It's like the lion in nature. This beast can be as magnificently dreadful a creature as any we could imagine. Come feeding time, lions go out on the plains, and they find food; and before there's food, there's death—the death of another creature—and that death is repeated over and over each day.

And yet after the lion's belly is full, it walks among prey with no harmful intent, and the prey knows it. Everything's cool. The lion goes down to the water hole to drink, you know, and a prey creature approaches the water and sees the lion there drinking. The antelope and gazelles know damn full well they're okay. Some instinct tells them, "Now listen, in the entire history of our species there hasn't been one of these guys here drinking with us who then attacked us; it's just not in the cards. So relax."

There's simply a certain order in the nature of things, and the animals operate accordingly. The natural laws are there, and the animals respond unfailingly. There are times when humanity operates the same way, in harmony with natural laws—and it's called *true progress*.

How come we were smart enough, without education or training but entirely on the basis of instinct and experience, to find a way to domesticate agriculture? Instead of having to follow the rains or the herds all the time as we once did, some enterprising soul said, "Wait a minute. You know something? These nuts and these fruit seeds and these grains—hmmm. Let's try this: let's put them in the soil." Then the tribe goes away and comes back nine months later and there's a field of grain, or a stand of trees.

The whole process of survival tells us that there's a morality to these natural rhythms, and that this morality is woven into the fabric of nature. For humanity, part of that fabric is the higher consciousness I was speaking of earlier. I feel that to aspire to that higher consciousness is to align ourselves with the natural order—in essence, to let go of the self. When we do this, when we rid ourselves of the petty little ego-drives that get in our way, we find ourselves much more in tune with the natural harmony, and good things can happen.

In the early sixties, director Ralph Nelson came upon a novel called *Lilies of the Field*, and he was so taken with it that he had an agent pursue the film rights. Then he found a screenwriter, and then he got in touch with me.

United Artists was the studio he went to, because he'd had successful relations with them before, but they weren't that enthusiastic about doing this small little picture about some nuns and a black handyman and faith and redemption. They were, however, interested in continuing their relationship with Ralph Nelson. The material was probably too soft for them, but in the interests of continuing their relationship, they offered him an outrageously small amount of money to make the film—240 thousand dollars.

That wasn't his salary. That was the entire budget for the film! *All* salaries, *all* production costs, *everything*.

And Ralph Nelson said yes! He put up his house as collateral, meaning that if he'd run over budget, he might very well have lost the place. We had no money in the budget for rehearsal, so he said to the actors, "We can rehearse, but you have to do it at my house, and we have to do it kind of secretly." This was because of the union rules and the fact that we weren't getting paid but were acting on . . . well, faith.

We rehearsed at his house in California for maybe a week, and then we flew to Arizona, checked into a motel, did the wardrobe thing, and started shooting the next day. Thirteen days later we were finished. Thirteen days later we had shot the entire film and were back in Los Angeles—from here to there and back again in two weeks.

Well, our faith was amply rewarded. For me, it meant winning the Academy Award for Best Actor. For all of us, it meant being a part of something that continues to touch people now, almost forty years down the road.

That picture had a lot to say about the kind of consciousness I aspire to, a consciousness that encompasses infinitely more than the world I see as I drive through Los Angeles at rush hour. But when the focus is entirely on the traffic, or on the appointment I'm rushing to, or on whatever else my petty problems may include, those manifestations of the ego are like the bright lights of a city that block out the stars. The stars are still there—I just can't see them.

But when I focus *beyond* the self, the interference drops away and suddenly I have access to a much grander form of awareness. It includes what I see and what I don't see but know to exist—even what will far outlast me as a physical being. I can begin to sense the connection of it all, and my place within it all, but only by removing myself from the center. In the moment that I do so, I know that this is Los Angeles, and that Los Angeles is part of a state, and that this state is part of the country, and that this country is part of a hemisphere, and that this hemisphere is part of a globe, and that this globe is one of nine or eleven (depending on your point of view) planets that move around the sun, and that the sun is one star, and that one star sits in a galaxy of 200 billion stars, and that this galaxy of 200 billion stars sits in a complex of 200 billion galaxies, and clusters of galaxies. I can even postulate alternative universes we don't know about yet. And all this is available to me when I sublimate the self—as is the full saga of hundreds of thousands of years of human evolution and human experience. When I cling to the self, I feel neurotic, alienated, insecure. It's when I let the self go that I can begin to realize how fully a part of this grand scheme I am and will always remain.

Which is another way of saying, "You are a child of the universe; you have a right to be here." Carl Sagan's first wife, Lynn Margulis, found another way to express the same idea through the concept of Gaia—the scientific view that our entire planet and all the ecosystems therein make up one organic whole, one living being that must be examined as such if we are to learn the way things truly are. "Mother Earth" is yet another, much older, and considerably less scientific way people have expressed the same thought.

To which I would add one postscript. I've read of studies done with youngsters—not with children, but with chimps—that have profound implications for our species and our life on this planet. The scientists behind this research know what it takes to raise a healthy baby chimp with a real mother—all the nutrition and the calories and so on. So they create a wire mother with maybe a bit of fur, a perch like an arm across the chest, and nipples that project through the wicker-and-wire mannequin. The nipples, attached to a sort of baby bottle, supply all the nutrients a chimp is known to need—the same nutrients that would come from a real mother's milk, maybe even more. But despite the fact that baby chimps can climb up on their "Wire Mothers" and be safe and get all the same nutrients, the same protein, the same basic protection from the elements they'd get from their real mothers, the chimps with the wire mothers wither and die.

My fear is this: I fear that as we cover more of our planet with concrete and steel, as we wire our homes with more and more fiber-optic cables that take the place of more intimate interactions, as we give our children more and more *stuff* and less and less time, as we go further and further away from the kind of simplicity I knew as a child on Cat Island, our Earth—Gaia or not—will become for us the Wire Mother, and our souls will wither and die as a result.

Every Sunday on Cat Island we would walk to the little church in Arthur's Town to attend mass. The service was Anglican Catholic, the Church of England. Then we would walk home, all the kids with our shoes slung over our shoulders by their laces—shoes not to be worn again for another week.

When we moved to Nassau we attended the Catholic Church, but this was more a matter of convenience than theology. The fact is the real religion in our lives was grounded in the old culture, a belief that there were always unseen forces at play in our lives, unexplainable mysteries that determined our fate.

All through my childhood, from my first understanding of words, I heard adults speaking of these unseen forces. I think my entire life has been in large part an effort to understand these "mysteries." I remember my father coming into the house one day and picking up an enamel plate. As he put it behind his back, he said, "I'm going to show you something, and I'm going to show it to you only once. Are you ready?" And then he brought the plate from behind his back. On it were hundreds of tiny fishes. Then he moved the plate behind his back again, and they were gone. I was astounded! I begged him to do it again, but he never would. This strange transformation was magic to me, and I never forgot it. It was a mystery that I puzzled over for years.

On leaving Cat Island, I began to encounter new concepts and values embedded in strange new words—words like *commerce* and *material success*. I had never heard of such things on Cat Island, but from Nassau and beyond they loomed large as matters of life and death. And yet the mysteries were no fewer in this modern, more commercial environment. What is physics but a repository of mysteries? And astronomy? My God! You talk about mysteries! The migration from culture to culture and through varying levels of technical sophistication doesn't matter. The mysteries shift their shapes, but the mysteries *remain*. God is the ultimate mystery, and fear of his wrath the ultimate driving force that governs how we behave.

When I was a kid in the Caribbean, there was a church on the next street from us. It was what was called a "Jumper church." Now, a Jumper church was the kind of church where, at every session, the minister would whip the congregation into a kind of psychological frenzy, which included jumping up from their seats to prance about in a trance while speaking in tongues.

Okay. I was witness to evenings like these. But being too young to really get a grasp on where these worshipers were coming from, I never understood the whole concept very well. But I felt that the worshipers were genuine. This "foreign tongue" I heard—which would be the equivalent of gibberish, I suppose—sounded genuine to me. It was like a long stutter. And never a word that sounded English.

These folks were on their feet, jumping around in peculiar movements and rambling on ecstatically, in this unknown tongue. Many of them would become so overwhelmed by the possession of themselves that they'd slip into a kind of jerking, epileptic-like fit. Once in that state, they would be cared for and nurtured back to normal by other members of the congregation (some who themselves had just passed successfully through the same ritual moments before, and others who in due time would likewise be drawn into the trance). By the end of the evening everybody would be sitting prim and proper in their chairs again.

At the end of the service people collected their fans—there was no air-conditioning in the church—and emptied out into the evening darkness, headed home. I remember observing their faces carefully as they were leaving, just as I had observed their behavior in their trance. Most of them I had known around the neighborhood, but I felt I didn't know them here.

Okay, now DISSOLVE. I'm a grown person now. Occasionally I travel back in my mind to such times. And still, to this day, I ask myself . . . unknown tongues? Were they, in fact, unknown tongues? If a recording were made at a service like that and the words spoken were stacked utterance for utterance against all the known languages of the world, what kind of similarities might appear? Or would the words turn out to be in a totally unknown tongue? Might the gibberish be found to be unique? And if it *did* turn out to be a totally unknown tongue, would it be a tongue unknown only to those of *us* who hear it? Could it be clear-as-a-bell communication in a place where it's understood? Could it be understood by God? Could there *be* a God? Can *you* be objective enough to perceive of there being a God who hears and understands *every* word?

"His eye is on the sparrow."

TEN

THE NATURE OF OPPOSITES

"WHO ARE YOU?" I once was asked when I was young. "I'm the me I chose to be," was my quick response. "Where did you come from, and how did you get here?" Equally glib responses waited on the tip of my tongue.

I'm no longer young now, and the season for summing up is descending upon me with steady insistence. So no further spin need be placed on answers to who I am or where I came from or how I got here. I am what I've become.

I came from a place of purity. I got here with the help of my friends, and my family, and perhaps the benign and protective influence of forces I'll never understand. I entered this world with the standard equipment of an average child, as was plain for all to see. Throughout my first ten years, my days were filled with the uneventful but traditional boychild developmental rituals of a semi-primitive society. Outside our island township the world at large didn't exist, except in snippets infrequently picked up from adult conversations.

In the next five years, the outside world introduced itself to me and instructed me as to where the lines were drawn: what the style of my behavior should be, where I should find a place to fit, and how I should rein in my expectations (never, ever reaching above the level approved for persons like me, if such meager dreams as I was allowed were to find accommodation).

The reining in of expectations was the centerpiece of the outside world's overall message, and it came through loud and clear. Limits had been defined, had been written into law and imposed on me long before I was even born. Therefore, I was forcefully advised to understand and accept that the burden would always be on me to see to it that my dreams were tailored to fit such width and breath as the limited expectations assigned me could comfortably entertain. While "expectations" meant "the sky's the limit" *for those favored*, that interpretation should never be expected to apply in cases like mine. I listened intently until each point had been driven home. Then I said, "Fuck you," in the nicest way I could.

By the end of those five years, the outside world and I had settled on what each could expect from the other. That each would keep an eye on the other had been a foregone conclusion. The outside world was annoyed and irritated by what it saw in me, but it was in no way fearful. Rather, it assumed that somewhere further on I would undoubtedly self-destruct. And there's the rub. In spite of the fact that we were ludicrously mismatched, I wasn't so afraid as *not* to question the world's power to determine what space I would be permitted to occupy. Nor would I allow it to impose a value of little consequence on my existence, or to reinforce its unyielding demand that its assessment of my value be my worth in the world at large. That power, which attempted to legislate how I should perceive myself in my own eyes, was unaware that, much earlier (long before I ever set sail for the outside world), roots sent down in a gentle place had taken hold. By the time the world and I took each other on, who and what I was had already been formed in my own eyes.

The ground had been broken and the seeds for this self had been sown somewhere inside me in a place called *imagination*. This was a word that had first appeared in otherwise familiar dialogue while my mother was administering one of the many whippings I was regularly accused of having earned.

"That imagination of yours [wham!] is going to get you in a bunch of trouble one of these days [wham! wham!] if you don't start listening [wham! wham! wham!) to what I tell you [wham! wham! wham! wham!]. Now get it into that thick head of yours once and for all [wham! wham! wham! wham! wham!] and start behaving yourself."

Imagination and whippings were two "blessings" always available to the young in that semi-primitive society, no less (I imagined) than in the larger world outside. In that beginning process the same imagination my mother feared would get me into trouble was also my host and guide on excursions into whatever my daydreams envisioned the world at large to be. Together, my imagination and my daydreams whetted my appetite for the wellspring of possibilities they had steadfastly promised would be there. Promises were all that was needed to get the process started in the child that I was, in the place where I lived, in the time of my boyhood. While reality and facts were not given to making promises, they were at the same time also disagreeable and dull and no match for the power of dreams.

Daydreams were guaranteed to please. They had it all over facts and reality when it came to getting groundwork done and foundations laid. However, daydreams were burdened with what in years to come would be revealed as their major weakness. Every ounce of the hard, grueling, exhaustive work necessary in the conversion from promises made to dreams fulfilled was the sole responsibility of the dreamer.

I have shown you, in broad strokes, who I was on Cat Island until I was ten and a half years old, and then in Nassau until fifteen, but contradictions abounded. The first time I lied, the first time I stole, the first time I cheated, my first blush of envy, flirtation with greed—not one of these vices was waiting at the docks in the new world to infect me upon my arrival there. I obviously had brought them with me from that gentle place I had left behind.

But where exactly did they come from? Were they in the genes of generations before, who had passed them quietly down? Or were they socialized behavioral responses, inescapable in human relationships?

I recall that as a youngster I was a killer of frogs and birds and a torturer of lizards. I recall that I fished for chickens with a straight pin bent into the shape of a hook. With a corn seed fixed on the tip as bait and the pinhook tied to a length of thread, I would cast among the chickens, then wait for one to pluck it up and swallow. I've killed fish and birds and discarded their bodies without having paid them the honor of eating their flesh. I can recall insects that, posing no threat, were squashed dead by a reflexive foot or hand of mine, long before *and* long after I had learned the meaning of the word *remorse*.

Cruelty was present in those acts, as was indifference. Was pleasure also in that mix? I can't say for sure. Maybe it was, and I edited out that awareness. Nor do I remember being the least bit impressed, at the time, by the ingenious architectural designs of those miraculous creations. Frogs. Birds. Lizards. Chickens. Fish. Insects. Not for one single, fucking moment did it enter my head. Or was I editing again? No. I don't think so.

It appears that we are all killers of one kind or another and that life begins in the darkness of a total ignorance that is peeled away slowly, little by little. What little we know eventually, we learn bit by bit. That sort of understanding wasn't likely to have been present in my earliest memories. Unless . . . ? Yes, unless everything I was ever to know was already there, lying layers deep in the darkness of my ignorance, waiting for layer after layer to be peeled away before the light of my memory could embrace it.

No evidence has surfaced in my adult recollections to support any notion that such a process lies beneath life's experiences. On the other hand, if by chance that notion is on the mark and the process is entirely true, then my earliest memories are still holding many secrets. Many answers.

Answers to questions like these: Is all that we've learned all that we know? If not, how much "knowing" do we possess that *wasn't* learned? If it's a substantial amount, how did we come to possess that which we didn't learn? Was the subconscious being fed by another source? Or was all the info simply prepackaged when the sperm hit the egg?

There are teenagers by the millions who could swear quite truthfully to having never, under any circumstances, stolen anything. Not me. If I had made that claim at the age of twelve, I would have perjured myself. By thirteen, other symbols of innocence had bitten the dust, and I was taking giant strides toward becoming a full-fledged rogue. All that after just two and a half years out there in that world at large. How much of my lying, cheating, and stealing might have been due, on the one hand, to the vibrating excitement that living on the edge can sometimes generate in the blood? On the other hand, how much might have been due to external contradictions I wasn't yet old enough to understand? Were the controls of my life not in my power as I had thought?

And if not, who or what could have been at those controls? Luck? Providence? Randomness? Nature's design?

Curiosity is one thing; wisdom is another. Maybe neither can fully cover the territory. Maybe one is meant to drive us, the other to beckon us. It's a question or an answer, boldly stated or subtlty implied, that gets me out of bed every morning. Curiosity is definitely a part of whatever energy brought me to where I am, good or bad. But wherever it is I am, it's for damn sure not a place of wisdom. I find myself, at this time in my life, no less challenged, no less plagued, no less intrigued, by what I still don't know.

Questions about my father, for instance, still haunt me. I've been led to believe, by the accounts of surviving contemporaries, that he was a bit of a rogue in his time.

"Reggie could hold his own with the best," said one old guy with a weather-beaten face.

"First-class rascal, first-class rogue," another chuckled.

"Know a couple old ladies still living who could tell you about your pa," volunteered a third, whose wizened eyes had held me locked in a long, level gaze.

I've plied those old buddies of Dad's with questions in an effort to see my father through their eyes. And I've compared that picture to the one drawn by the dictionary's description of a rogue: "a dishonest, knavish person; scoundrel; a playfully mischievous person; scamp; a tramp or vagabond."

The dictionary's version of a rogue misses my father by a mile. His old buddies' version speaks of behavior in a time I never knew. Was he a good man? A loving father? Yes, I think so. But he was other things as well, and now I must try to know him in full for all that he was in the time of his life.

A seriously flawed man and a loving father are often one and the same person. In some cultures, where "faithful husbands" are anything but monogamous, a highly specific definition as to what constitutes fidelity has allowed men to escape condemnation. My father, thanks to that narrowest of definitions, was an escapee in the culture of Cat Island. So was the local priest. Lots of farmers. Loads of fishermen. Schoolteachers, shopkeepers, house-builders, and well-diggers. All declared "faithful husbands" by a definition with roots in ancient cultures whose wives and mothers had no say. Handed down through thousands of years, picking up strength along the way, that definition has left room for mistresses, open affairs on the side, even polygamy. That narrowest of definitions has declared a faithful husband to be one who can be depended upon to provide for his wife and children. Any man who has met that narrow test has been beyond reproach for any other behavior resulting from uncontrolled drives and passions.

By that one-sided and far too generous definition, my father, along with millions of others since the dawn of time, was granted forgiveness never earned, never deserved.

I've wrestled with questions about my father's character in part because I'm still wrestling with my own. And that battle has taught me that if the image one holds of one's self contains elements that don't square with reality, one is best advised to let go of them, however difficult that may be.

A few years ago I was required to undergo surgery for prostate cancer. In the weeks before surgery my most important concern was waking up cancer-free, but a close second was preserving my image. I hate like hell to admit any weakness or failure. What would the press say if the prognosis was poor?

But surgery left me naked to myself and to the world, with prostate *and* camouflage removed. Shortcomings, weaknesses,

frailties, vulnerabilities, inadequacies, self-doubts, and all—
my total reality in plain sight. No less flawed than most, and no
longer burdened by the need to appear otherwise.

At every point through all the years before, the greatest
threat to my life's program had been my fear of failure. Not failure itself, mind you, but my *fear* of failure. And now, once the
surgery had been scheduled, I managed to translate the publicity that I knew would result into a full-scale, worldwide failure
thing. I had enjoyed so many successes over the years that my
lifelong fear of failure had been relegated to the subbasement.
But it had remained alive and well down there, ready to come
out with a roar with the cancer diagnosis. With blunt honesty,
my cancer said, "You're not a 'star'; you're a human being, vul-
nerable like all the rest." My whole existence up to that point
had been based on the mantra, "I will be better; I will be better;
I *am* better." Now this life-threatening disease demanded that I
face the hypocrisy of that charade.

In the months that followed the removal of my prostate, I
grew to see myself as a combination of things, and a recipient of
many blessings—not the least of which were the influences of
luck, timing, and all of the other "mysteries" that went into the
making of my life. Though one can never put one's finger on
such intangibles, one nevertheless knows that they're real and
are definitely a part of the mix.

I'm a person who's never lost sight of appreciation for anything I've had above subsistence. When I went to pick up my
first check as an actor in a film, I was afraid that the studio
would see the truth, which was that I was so happy to be acting

that if I'd had the money and they'd asked me, I would have paid them for the privilege.

I still watch money, having learned the hard way, and I spend it with a certain mindfulness. I try to be *reasoned* in my dealings with money, because somewhere inside myself I've always been afraid that I'll be judged unworthy of it. With me always are recollections of lines from the early years—lines like, "Ah, well, they haven't caught up with me yet."

I often heard another kind of comment as well during those early years. People would say things like, "You get *paid* for this?" (I still hear that one.) Or people would say, "How ya doin'?" and answer, "Not bad for colored." Later, I would discover how many meanings that last comment carried in the black community. Among other things, it was a bonding expression born out of racial matters and widely used as a reminder of all the dreams shared in common. That's the way it was. "Are you workin' hard, or are you hardly workin'?" Big answer: "Doin' all right"—and keeping a straight face was a part of it. *Oh*, my life and days, yes, in ways subtle and otherwise, a scarcity of money goes a long way in shaping the vocabulary of a community.

A sobering rediscovery of an awareness I had relinquished to denial came back to me with jolting clarity when I was in the postsurgery stage. That awareness was that I had come to believe a little bit in my own press clippings. Having been a principal player in motion pictures for a very long time, mine was considered a successful career, and certainly it has provided a good living for my family and me. I've received plenty of recognition, and I'm well thought of throughout a sizable portion of the world. Moreover, I've become closely identified with several of the parts I've played—uplifting, interesting, positive, good guys, brave and with dignity. You can't receive (and enjoy) those kudos and that kind of acceptance without some of it going to your head. A little bit, anyway. And if you keep hearing it, somewhere along the way you start accepting it as the truth. I had, in fact, reached that point. I enjoyed believing much of the praise I heard. It brought me good feelings of acceptance. Feelings of worthiness, usefulness. I was thought of as someone with a gift, a skill, a craft. And one that hadn't been wasted or abused.

Bathed in all that praise, I had lost touch with my own personal measure of myself, a more realistic assessment that incorporated the weaknesses and foibles, the generosity and the darkness, the human vulnerability. There were even times, during bouts of doubt and depression and feelings of inadequacy, that I found myself giving the public image a boost. While manipulating and inflating that image, I would ease my conscience by referring to my actions as a gentle massage necessary for the sake of maintenance.

There are different kinds of strength, you know? My parents weren't people of great power, commanding huge resources. Much of the time they simply clung to life on an island that could have been reclaimed by the sea at any moment. But they carried on with great dignity, and they accomplished much. There was a kind of strength in their existence that I hadn't been forced by difficult circumstances to practice. But now, with cancer and an uncertain future looming, I knew that the moment had found me. I couldn't *not* try to summon their strength. I knew that if I was going to die as a result of this disease, I had to find the strength to face death with some dignity, some courage, and some acceptance of the inevitable. Some honesty. Especially when I had to say to my wife, "Here are the possibilities." In preparing her as best I could, I tried to let her know that I was concerned but not panicked, so that she would gain strength from that to carry her through whatever would be the outcome.

———

WHEN I WAS quite young, with no awareness of the personal demons within me or the different forms and faces those demons could endlessly assume, I developed a belief system that was fraught with danger. I had come to believe that the hard work of good, honest, fair-minded people with a passionate commitment to justice would bring about a world in which a life of dignity for all would be the rule. A world in which opportunities to pursue fulfillment would be limited only by the outer margins of one's individual ability. I had come to believe that problems of race, ethnicity, color, education, sexual preference, class, and poverty, and the attendant afflictions left in their wake to plague the modern world in their names, would be successfully resolved through the efforts of those same good, honest, fair-minded people. A new progressive force with insight and cohesion was in the making, thought I. The ills of my generation would ultimately be addressed.

Frictions would be tamed, tensions neutralized, and out of the hearts and minds of good men and women would come the way to a better future—one in which we would all lend a hand at weaving the strong cultural threads of our social diversity into a more caring, a more *human*, community.

Bullshit!

At eighteen I was plenty old enough to damn well know better than that. And if it sounds like I've rendered a self-assessment far too harsh in light of my age, trust me, I haven't. I was *wrong* to embrace that crap. Spending my impressionable years operating in the real world on such wishful thinking wasn't only too costly, it was also too dangerous. I well remember as a young man learning day by day to test my wings in life by stepping farther and farther away from my ignorance. Then one day, at a bold distance from the safety of that ignorance, I finally spotted my demons—first one, then another, then another.

Some people don't want to know of the presence of personal demons; they pretend not to know even when they *do* know. And there are others whose consciousness merely dances around the edges of their dark-side reality all their lives. Those folks never step close enough to look even one demon in the eye.

But listen, the day one decides to take the reins of one's own life into one's own hands, to captain one's own ship, that's the day the dance around the edges starts to slow down, bringing that person to a place where gnawing questions will no longer lie still. To a place where one just can't help wondering why so often in life an obvious solution to a problem gets twisted and pulled into a knot of frustration, with no regard for logic or reason. To a place where one finds oneself more and more at a loss to explain why logic and reason themselves so often go down in defeat at the hands of energies that are negative, hostile, destructive, and cruel.

I don't remember exactly when I began to ask myself those questions that "wouldn't lie still," but when I did, they led to endless face-to-face encounters between myself and the dark side of my own nature—that part of me that has always been there, saying to my deaf ears, "I'm here, and one day you'll be ready to take me into account. On that day you're gonna *have* to take me into account. You aren't ever going to manage through your life without coming by me."

Age-old speculation as to whether the dark side is full-blown in some people and almost nonexistent in others or is distributed more widely—some in everyone—rages still from generation to generation. I personally think that there's some darkness in everyone, though the "some" varies as widely as do personality profiles in the family of man. Darkness can explode in nuclear proportions with disastrous consequences or make itself felt in small, subtle, irritating ways, depending on the day, the time, the hour, the situation, and who's in the room.

The extent of the dark side isn't easy to fathom. People who kill aren't evil twenty-four hours a day, and the dark side doesn't advertise. The dark side in each of us operates from behind masks of varying complexity, coming to the fore when we elect to use its services. We all have a reservoir of rage, dissatisfaction, self-loathing, unhappiness, intolerable feelings of inadequacy. But we don't necessarily express these things. They're veiled, hidden from ourselves as much as from others. But whether hidden or not, they make us all capable of terrible things. And the evil that we're capable of enacting doesn't flourish only in moments of rage or revenge, or in response to some unspeakable offense. Sometimes horrible acts are entertained and allowed under very considered and thought-through circumstances. "Everybody is entitled to a job," someone might say, "but not *my* job. You try to take *my* job and I'll kill you!"

Sometimes the violence in the dark side is turned inward. Some people take pills; some jump out the window. But whether violence is turned inward or outward, people can't isolate components of their rage—it's an accumulation. We think we're raging against the darkness, but in fact we're struggling against a life we can't control. We opt to struggle for balance rather than fight chaos. "What got into him?" people ask of a well-mannered neighbor who turned ballistic. "He isn't that kind of guy."

But *of course* he is! We're *all* that kind of guy! Do I have the wherewithal to be a violent person? Or course I do. I could do unspeakable things to protect my children. Would that be a choice made at that precise moment? Yes. But where would I go for that intensity? Into what well of murderous impulses would I dip? That reservoir has to be there already, waiting.

For me this awareness was the beginning of a new perception of self, of others, and of the world around me. In light of my growing understanding, I took aggressive steps to try to find out why my best efforts had so often been defied by problems I would have thought were fixable. I boldly peeked inward—saw nothing I understood—then retreated again to ponder where inside myself I should look for answers to external human problems that defy one's best efforts. I spent much time looking in the wrong places, but even there I came away with lessons. For example, some things simply *aren't* going to get better. And some people just refuse to learn; if learning isn't *good* for them, doesn't *profit* them, they're not interested.

So what else should that worldview have encompassed? Having grown up in an idyllic place that I mistakenly believed held the whole story if I could just discern it, my determination to find the answer to that question pulled me into a process that led to discovery.

The first conclusion that struck me was that the pace toward "progress" was slower than it should be. Growing increasingly impatient with that pace, I observed it closely and found out that the problem wasn't *pace* but *direction*. I concluded that other people and other forces weren't just going slowly; they were trying to go *another way, other places altogether*. There were parts of me as well—of *every* individual—that were trying to go other places altogether.

I also drew some conclusions about the educability of human beings. I had tended to believe in the essential nobility of man, had seen man as Noble Beast, and had thought that *education* could bring about change. Anything good and necessary that wasn't happening was missing, I had thought, because of someone who *didn't understand yet*. But I came to believe that, while there are in fact some people who haven't yet been shown, there are far more who are never, ever going to see, regardless of *what* they're shown, and how often.

I also concluded that what it is we need to see—that Big Answer we all seek—is *even more complex* than it appears to be. More than a value system and its opposite held in degrees by various people. More than the vague but persistent sense that somewhere in ourselves lie hidden such answers as would be appropriate to questions we're not yet fearless enough to ask. Questions like, for instance, How much truth is there in the lingering suspicion that Nature is fooling with us? Are we principal players with pivotal roles in her scenario (as we fervently hope) or merely inconsequential afterthoughts with not the slightest impact on her agenda (as we often fear)?

Why do we spend most or all of our lives searching for balance between the bewildering variety of opposites designed in Nature's nature? Why do we struggle so hard to find a comfort zone between up and down, in and out, here and there, this and that, him and her, us and them, high and low? Ever present is this *duality*, and ever present is our need to articulate ourselves betwixt the various poles.

I concluded, finally, that in the juxtaposition of energies, Nature's intent was major: the idea of the Other. The definition of self by its opposite: "I am not that." I further concluded that if such duality in so many aspects of her being was necessary to Nature's sense of herself, her sustenance, her continuance, her survival, then duality must be a fundamental circumstance in her overall design. It must represent a basic, basic truth: *that collision is essential, that opposites create an energy, and that maybe nature has no preference for either of the opposites.* (What arrogance we possess, then, to think that there's a preference in favor of *our* side!)

Instead, Nature waits for us to discover that her focus is on the energy that ensues from the coming together of yin and yang, and the coming together of high and low, and the coming together of this and that, and the coming together of us and them. All that blood on *Wild Kingdom*—we accept it in the animal world. In *our* world we say, "It's dog eat dog," and it sounds like a bad thing; but we talk about the "food chain" on the Serengeti Plain and give it civilized acceptability with polished terms like *zoology.*

During a bull session one evening, wrestling with this issue over after-dinner coffee, my buddy Charley Blackwell said to me, "You know, we're not talking just about a process *in* nature, we're talking about a process that might be Nature itself." I took this to be a warning for us not to take ourselves too seriously. We were, after all, just two guys with little more than a fair amount of curiosity trying to stretch our minds by chewing on an issue light-years bigger than our bite, he seemed to be saying. I signaled my accord with that cautionary sentiment, and also its use as a ground rule to cover the deeper discussion that was likely to come.

At that point he reached into his knapsack and hauled out his trusted little tape recorder, positioned it on the table, and said, "Okay, let's see where this Nature's-use-of-opposites thing leads."

"You first," said I.

"Okay," said he.

"Let's look at it in the same light as if it were the New Testament/Frank Capra/USA/Judeo-Christian dream that sustained us growing up and for a great deal of our adult lives. Then we found out that the dream *was* a dream, that it was inaccurate and incomplete. But we also discovered that that dream, *and the inaccuracy of it,* had kept us alive and allowed us to survive. *All* of us believed in John Wayne. Later on we said, 'Well, he's a conservative.' But the essential 'winning through,' and 'By God, we'll get there,' and 'Over the hill, huh?' and 'Work hard and you'll get there,' and 'Be true and loyal,' and all those other things—*that's* what kept us going. Now, knowing that—that (a) the dream kept us going and (b) it isn't true— what do we tell the children? Do we tell them to keep the Capra? Let them find out the truth for themselves? Or do we tell them—?"

Here I interrupted. "Would what we now perceive as truth be so tough for them to handle?" I asked. "Why *not* share with them what we've observed? Tell them it appears that Nature doesn't give doodley-squat about the whites and the blacks and the browns and the blues. That on the evidence, she looks to be operating in her own best interests, and *we*, as best as can be told, are a part of how *she* operates and *not* vice versa. That we believe her to have no preference between opposites but feel that her focus falls sharpest on the clashing of opposing forces in mutual annihilation. If we speak of basic facts, truths, constant realities that are forever there, then of course a lot of dreams *will* be stripped away, sending Capra and John Wayne right out the window. But how bad is that? If the children hear our thoughts about opposing forces in mutual annihilation providing energy by which Nature perpetuates herself, *and* they learn, thereby, that the browns, the blues, the whites, the blacks, and whatever combinations there are will continually go clash! flash! slash! wham! bang! boom! *and not know why*—then those children will be the better for it. Otherwise, they might grow up to hear each other exclaim, 'Oh, my God. Jesus Christ, these people don't understand! Why can't we get them to learn? Why can't we get them to see? We've got to *show* them.' And they would remain unaware that Nature sees all, while her interest encompasses only the sparks that fly."

"Right," Charley conceded. "But if you'd known that truth when you were a kid, before you left for Nassau, would that truth have taken away from the hope that kept you alive? What we're *really* talking about is Santa Claus. We know there's no Santa Claus, but we're grown up. We're talking about *when* we let the children become aware that there's no Santa Claus."

"Hope, Charley, is always born out of the same womb. It doesn't matter what your level is. If you're a child, your hope comes from the place where your imagination and your little bit of knowledge tell you that things are most favorable. Where you get comfort, warmth, kisses; where you get cared for. Where you get fed. Your hope is all intertwined with that. With the people who do the feeding, when they feed you, how they feed you, how they protect you from the elements, and so on. *But*—take that child to ten or twelve years old and share with him our adult speculations about Nature, about what Nature does and how it operates, and that child—then— would have to begin to articulate his or her hopes and dreams on the basis of *that* understanding."

I paused for breath. "In other words, hopes and dreams are necessary tools to the survival instinct. With the acceptance of new truths, hopes and dreams become subject to rewriting according to the needs of the new reality. On the other hand, hopelessness sneaks about on the periphery of our lives, wait- ing to close in on us behind certain truths. It's watched and held in check at a safe distance by our instinct to survive. Of course, when hopelessness succeeds in narrowing the distance enough to infect hopes and dreams and slowly sap their strength, then the instinct to survive falters. Begins to wear down. And if it's ever subdued to a point where it can no longer churn out the stuff from which dreams are spun to give flight to hope, then one resigns oneself to what follows. And, over time, hopeless- ness lays claim to another victim. But, as the old saying goes, 'As long as there's life, there's hope.'"

"Is that an assumption?" Charley asked.

"As long as there's life, there's hope?"

"Yeah."

"Well, you have to qualify the line," I said. "As long as there's a *chance* for the life you envision—and so on."

"And hope isn't *planted* in us?" inquired Charley. "It isn't a vision given to us as we grow up, by surroundings such as movies, patriotic books, attitudes of people around us, you know?—what Studs Terkel called the 'good war'?"

"Yeah, it's planted some, but it's there from the beginning too. I think it shares a primal bond with pleasure."

"I'm talking about general, basic hope," said Charley. "You know, Hope 101. The hope that is a kind of belief that things, people, conditions, *whatever* can get better."

"That hope is constant, Charley, but let's examine what we mean by 'things.' And what do we mean by 'better'? We have to define 'better' as well."

I took a moment to marshal my thoughts. "Let's go back to the time when we were unaware that Nature might be operating the way we now suspect she does. At that point, hope was qualitatively different. But now, when we assume, as we do, the possibility that Nature doesn't give doodley-squat beyond the flying sparks that are important to her sustenance, we then say, 'Hey, wait a minute. What is it that *I* want? The hell with Nature; she's getting hers. What is it that *I* want? Well, I want a better life.'

"Okay," I continued. "Before you can achieve a better life, you've got to be able to spell out what a better life means. What it means *for you*. Not for your neighbor or the white guy across the tracks. For *you*. You're probably going to say, 'A better life is *more comforts*. And those comforts are of a great variety. I want to be more comfortable *emotionally*. I want to be more comfortable *physically*. I want to be more comfortable *psychologically*.

More comfortable with myself. With my neighbors. In my consciousness of myself and my existence. Aside from comfort, I want to feel good. I want to feel good about things.'"

Charley nodded agreement and poured another cup of coffee.

"Okay, *what* things?" I pressed. You might say, 'I want to feel good about what goes on around me. I want to feel good about the way I'm thought of. The way I think of myself. Good about how my friends see me and how they feel with me and how they accept me. I want to feel good about the things I do. For myself and for my children, for my wife, my friends and my community. I want to feel good in other ways too. I want to feel *pleasurably* good. Ideally, I would like life to be as close to an orgasm as it can get.' And who wouldn't?

"So my call is this: hope essentially is goal-oriented. And however else one may define hope, there's no denying the likelihood that comfort, feeling good, and pleasures are basic ingredients in the stuff that hope spins into dreams. Therefore, when hope attains an occasional goal, a dream or part of a dream is realized, causing us to feel that much 'better' about our lives. How much is due to hope implanted by books and movies and how much to inborn urges and instincts whose natural orientation is toward the pursuit of pleasure? If a harder look at 'things' and 'better' doesn't provide a satisfactory answer, it should at least give us a clearer view of how hope matches up to reality and how dreams keep us keeping on."

Charley looked at me a moment, then asked, "Now that we're here, looking back across our years—the children; what shall we tell them about our journey? What shall we tell them about ourselves?"

"The truth," I said without hesitation.

"That life is tough?"

"Life *is* tough, damn right!"

ELEVEN

THE MEASURE
OF A MAN

IN THE PROFESSIONAL theater, audiences are known to have been swept out of their individual realities and transported to imaginary places and to imaginary times that appear as real as any place or time out of their own experience. I once was well acquainted with such occurrences. On more than a few such occasions I was present, on one side of the footlights or the other, when actors and audience conspired to make magic. Time and again I witnessed some unknown force take hold and keep us transfixed to the evening's end, then release us gently and send us home with gifts of remembrances to last for a lifetime.

For me, over the decades, much of the purity gradually

faded from that process, giving way to a tolerable sameness. I had a film career to manage, as well as a directing career, a family to raise, business to take care of. And as I grew older, the events on my calendar began to take on a more retrospective flavor. Testimonial dinners and award ceremonies, sometimes for colleagues, sometimes for myself, documentaries and interviews as film historians and others looked back to recapture some essence of my time in Hollywood. It was as if I had become a living repository, and not much more.

Then, a few years ago, on an early spring evening at the Mark Taper Forum in Los Angeles, the magic of theater returned in full bloom for me. Actress Anna DeVere Smith was onstage in a solo performance, and as I sat mesmerized, I surrendered completely to her craftsmanship. She had so captured the imagination of the audience that we were all a living part of the world she had created on that Mark Taper stage. She had convinced us that all the magic laid out in front of us was real.

When the final curtain fell, I was elated. In addition to the pleasure of the experience, I also felt a hunger—one that had lain dormant for years—suddenly begin to gnaw inside me.

Out of the power of her artistry, one actress alone populated that stage with a variety of characters and brought to life settings that could be seen only through the eyes of the imagination and touched only by the finger of wonder. Throughout the evening she had complete command of my senses. And for good reason: she had taken me back to times that had slipped from memory.

Early in my struggling years as an actor I had no knowledge of the word *pantomime*. When I was introduced to it in an acting class, I was intrigued by its complexity. To tell a story without words—to convey physically all the nuances of tragedy, comedy, and drama (nuances that would ordinarily be illuminated by words)—appeared to me to be creativity of a very special kind. It wasn't long before I began to devise comic pantomimes and present them in acting class, with encouraging results. Soon I had developed a repertoire good enough to roll out at parties as entertainment for friends. My confidence at pantomime would grow steadily in the following two years. I actually began fantasizing about honing my sketches into a nightclub routine.

Soon enough, however, the idea of pantomime and nightclubs was abandoned in the wake of a gathering film career that would eventually absorb my focus to the exclusion of all else. Left beneath the swirling shadows of Hollywood's intoxicating promise, such notions withered and faded, slowly slipping from memory's reach to lie dormant for decades. Then, that night at the Mark Taper, they suddenly reawakened as part of a creative explosion at the center of my consciousness. They came to life in a cluster of long-forgotten, unfulfilled desires that I had abandoned and left to perish, along with once-strong urges that had been either unmet or ignored so long that they too had faded or crumbled into dust. "So much had been dreamed of," I thought to myself. "So much had been left undone."

Then, like a bolt out of the blue, came a realization. It was something I never, ever should have forgotten. A credo, a deeply held conviction, a challenge in waiting. For most of my life in films and theater I had believed that an actor should repeatedly seek to have his measure taken by challenges inherent in his craft. Every actor should aim always toward earning a place among those privileged members of his profession who are considered by most to be creative, artistic, and suited to their calling. I had always known that the very best way for me to improve self and craft was to continually test my limits. And I knew, on that evening of my realization—I was in my mid-sixties at the time—that the ideal way to do that would *still* be to walk out onto an empty stage, face an audience alone, and for two hours spin words, talent, skill, and craft into magic enough to seduce that audience into my imagination, and have them invite me into theirs.

All through my career I had been driven by a huge need to stay on my toes, in life as well as on the stage. Backed by the brashness of youth and a recklessness of thought, that need was translated into a warning that was always with me: "Don't be as good as, be better than; raise the risk level." Vague recollections suggest that I even managed, on occasion, to forge discipline out of resolve.

But looking back from the distance of that early spring evening at the Mark Taper, I realized that I had forgotten all that. I had tarried too long in places where success had tempted me into *lowering* my risk level. But at least I could still feel the need to rattle this cage of my own making. Before the evening was over, that need came rushing forth as the powerful urge to step on a stage, face an audience, and test my limits once again.

Revitalized and pulsating, the old theatrical impulse I had first met at the American Negro Theatre came charging upward to flex itself in the presence of all the magic it sensed being spun everywhere around us. It also came to take a look at me and once again vibrate through my body. And in that reawakening, the impulse was as forceful as I had ever known it to be— which was, of course, a reassuring surprise.

There it was, that old compulsion standing in the wings. We recognized each other instantly. It hadn't changed, as far as I could tell. It was still dangerous. I knew that it would demand of me the same commitment it had required years before. In looking each other over, we both could see that I had changed. With age I had grown increasingly cautious, and over time I had conveniently forgotten about that old bond between us. How *could* I have forgotten how much we had in common? Forgotten how often I had been attracted and repulsed at the same time? Forgotten how often in my dreams we had teamed up and scored? Now that old compulsion had returned to stare back at me from the center of my conscious-ness. I felt its power reaching out to me. Trying to take hold. Yet I felt comfortable in my distance. Still capable of standing my ground.

In the magic of that evening, the flirtation began exactly where it had left off when I was young and unafraid of looking inward in search of whatever I might find—when something living in the darkness was discovered tugging at the sleeves of my imagination. And our flirtation moved quickly to action, as flirtations often do.

On that evening at the Mark Taper, I decided that there could be no better time than that moment for me to explore the long-forgotten, unfulfilled urge that had once possessed me. To engage compulsion on all matters of unfinished business between us. To look around inside myself at roadways that had once seemed to lead nowhere in particular and ask why they had been dead-ends. What was it about those roadways? Were they overwhelmed by challenges too great? Were they intercepted by risks too high? Were they restrained by regrets too painful? Or was it me? Maybe it was *me*. Maybe I was in denial of fears I didn't have the courage to face.

Now that I'm older, with fewer axes to grind, I suspect that certain roadways that seemed to lead nowhere weren't the dead-ends I saw, but simply roads marked with warning flares saying that some personal failure was destined to occur. On the other hand, I can't help wondering whether, had I persevered, *some* of those roadways might have been the very paths I should have traveled most. Maybe along those untraveled pathways I would have found important lessons waiting to be learned.

Still, to step onstage in a professional theater at my age to do a one-man show with voice, body, and mind as my only tools was clearly a risky business. "You must be nuts," I told myself on the way home, as the magic of Anna DeVere Smith began to wear off.

Over the next few weeks I attempted a sober, practical, objective, clearheaded analysis of the pros and cons. I realized that whatever force was drawing me nearer to this sizable undertaking had origins too troublesome to untangle. After a full month, I still hadn't been able to shake off the magic of the theater or regain a safe distance from my old friend compulsion. The cautious side of me resisted this business of walking on the edge—especially now, at a time when a fall was likely to be fatal. The wild side of me, on the other hand, was ready to accept the fact that high gains require high risks.

In the end I agreed with the wild side and resolved to go forward on the basis of two compelling reasons. First, I needed to settle obligations owed to self. Second, in the process I wanted to spin enough magic to close out what had been for me a genuinely magical career.

Like a fighter in training, I started preparing for the event. I watched other actors in other theaters do solo evenings. I researched actors and textual material from successful productions in the past. I paid attention to details, adjusted my social calendar, carved out a preliminary timeframe, cleared my desk. But the two most basic issues remained unresolved. Who would write such an evening, and what would be the nature of the material?

I put this question to my friend Charley Blackwell, whom I had met in the late fifties, not long after he'd arrived in New York from Philadelphia to pursue his dreams. Like young unknowns before him, he went to New York to conquer Broadway as a dancer. But the times were insensitive and the pickings were lean. Race was a factor, and denial was comfortably in control of virtually all questions concerning race in the America of those days.

Though he would dance with both the Pearl Primus and Geoffrey Holder companies, times came early on when he had to sell cigarettes from the Philip Morris company to cover the rent. Once when things were at their bleakest, George Mills, a fellow dancer, asked Charley to accompany him as a drummer on an audition for an upcoming musical called *Fanny*, to be directed by Joshua Logan and produced by David Merrick. George Mills didn't get the job, but Joshua Logan and David Merrick saw something in the drummer. Enough to offer him a job in the show—a spot that would make use of his dancing talent. The show was a hit. Charley Blackwell was launched. But not as a dancer. David Merrick was impressed with his quickness of mind, his critical thinking abilities, and his overall grasp of the technical nature of live theater.

During the next twenty years, Charley would move through the ranks in the Merrick organization to become a master stage manager. He went on to England to direct the Merrick productions of *Promises, Promises* and *One Hundred and Ten in the Shade*. After that he wrote the book for the Broadway musical *The Tap Dance Kid*. And then he wrote the movie *A Piece of the Action*, for my company, and rewrote *Stir Crazy* for Columbia Pictures, which I was privileged to direct. Along the way he had written two additional movie scripts for my company, so I knew of no better person for the job at hand now.

I laid out the plan to Charley, but he said he had commitments and obligations that could be long-term. When asked *how* long-term, he gave me a vague response that suggested a reluctance to clarify. "When and if I can work through everything that's on my desk at the moment," he said, "I'll call you." Strange, I thought. But I left it to rest and turned my mind to the unwelcome task of finding a possible substitute.

For many weeks I searched through a mental list of all the writers I knew, as well as others I knew only by reputation. Meanwhile, I compiled notes in case the search ended on my own doorstep. Could *I* write a one-man show, to be performed by me, fashioned out of material each piece of which would be a living part of my own life? Yes, but not like Charley Blackwell could.

As more weeks passed and more notes accumulated, I saw with increasing clarity what a monumentally formidable task stood before me. However, I had no choice but to press on.

Late one morning the phone rang. I picked it up, and it was Charley. "How ya doin'?" he asked in a cheery voice.

"Fine," I said, delighted to hear from him.

"Well, I'm clear now. You still want to do that thing?"

"Yes! Yes! *Hell*, yes," I replied.

"Well, I'm ready," he said.

What he *didn't* say, and what I didn't know, was that in the months prior to our last conversation, doctors had discovered cancer in his bladder. Surgery followed, during which prostate cancer was also discovered and dealt with.

We went to work, yet all the while Charley kept his illness to himself. There was no telltale behavior, and the ostomy bag he wore under his clothing to collect his urine wasn't apparent to any of us. Charley Blackwell was just as I'd always known him. Halfway through the project, my doctors saw warning signs in my blood that maybe *my* prostate should be watched. Many ultrasounds and four biopsies later, they pinpointed the cancer. It was only then, in an effort to comfort me, that Charley revealed *his* history. I underwent surgery for the removal of my prostate on June 3, 1993.

When I was again able to work, we resumed, each of us hoping that the next five years would show no sign of our cancer's return. Months later, we had a completed project. The entire evening was going to be material from my life. Nothing outside of my experiences would be added. We were relieved to have finished and were enthusiastic about the results.

Charley went back to New York with a copy of the script that we both agreed should be given to a producer friend of his, someone whom I, too, held in high regard. Here's where dreams would meet reality—the project's first exposure to objective scrutiny. Despite all our years in the business, we were both wired with anxiety and hopefulness.

Then the reaction came. Not good.

Charley and I were disappointed, but we swallowed hard and digested the details. Finally, it came home to us that we had made a mistake in the selection of the source material. We were forced to admit that the material should have been taken not from *my* life but rather from life itself. We resolved to return to the drawing board with this new point of view.

Charley and I didn't see much of each other over the next several months, a time spent mostly in note-gathering. Early one evening he dropped by to visit with my wife and me at our New York apartment and to report on his progress. An hour later we shared a cab with him across town. My wife and I were on our way to the theater; Charley was on his way to somewhere else. At 97th Street and Columbus Avenue he got out. We said our goodbyes, and we never saw him again. The cancer had returned. He died on June 2, 1995.

Sometimes it seems that when crushing losses are the reality, a resistant mechanism springs into action to protect the mind from instant overload, mercifully allowing for the gradual absorption of invasive and toxic information. Charley Blackwell was no more. He had slipped into what W.E.B. Du Bois once called "that long deep and endless sleep." Needless to say, the world we knew hung heavy in the days and months that followed.

After the magnitude of the loss had hit home and family and friends were finally able to turn the corner toward healing, I drifted back to the "material in progress." I remember thinking of it at the time more as "material in shambles," due to Charley's untimely departure.

As to questions that remain standing in the face of humanity's relentless pursuit of answers, maybe Nature arranges it to her benefit that some of us set out on journeys that can have no end. Consider, for a moment, that the amount of energy spent by human beings in pursuit of something that doesn't exist might, in very real terms, represent a sizable chunk of the energy Nature needs to make the world go 'round. Which might also explain why—even after a lifetime of struggle— most of us never find the rainbow we promised ourselves would lead us to our pot of gold.

Charley never lived to see our dream fulfilled. The same cancer that declined to take me called him back to Nature. I don't know why he died any more than I know why I went from being a stargazer on the beaches of Cat Island to an actor in Hollywood. But I *do* know that I'm responsible not for what happens but for what I make of it. It's up to me to take my own measure, to claim what's real, to answer for myself.

I'm still here, and truth be told, the compulsion to create and express is still here. Our first efforts at a one-man show met with failure, and oh, how I hate to fail. My colleague has succumbed, and to an illness that I've shared, which is at times doubly dispiriting. But I still dream of that final moment onstage.

Surely this must be the highest-stakes game of all. And maybe the oracles are trying to tell me that this is one I can't win. That my survival instincts aren't going to help me this time. That I won't be able to charm this opponent into neutral, no matter how much drive and hard work and talent I apply. But there's still a beating heart at the center of my being, and while there's life . . .

Human life is a highly imperfect system, filled with subordinate imperfections all the way down. The only thing we know for sure is that in another eight billion years it will all be over. Our sun will have spent itself; and the day it expires, you'll hear the crunch all over this solar system, because then everything will turn to absolute zero.

But you can't live focused on that. You can't hang on to that. Anyway, luckily we puny individuals have only seventy-five or eighty-two or ninety-six years to look forward to, which is still a snap in the overall impenetrableness of time. So what we do is we stay within the context of what's practical, what's real, what dreams can be fashioned into reality, what values can send us to bed comfortably and make us courageous enough to face our end with character.

That's what we're seeking. That's what it's all about, you know? We're all of us a little greedy. (Some of us are *plenty* greedy.) We're all somewhat courageous, and we're all considerably cowardly. We're all imperfect, and life is simply a perpetual, unending struggle against those imperfections.

INDEX

Sidney Poitier was the first African-American actor to win the Academy Award for best actor for his outstanding performance in *Lilies of the Field* in 1963. He has starred in over forty films, directed nine, and written four. His landmark films include *The Defiant Ones*, *A Patch of Blue*, *Guess Who's Coming to Dinner* and *To Sir, With Love*. Among his many accolades, he has been selected as the thirty-sixth recipient of the Screen Actors Guild's highest honour, the Life Achievement Award for an outstanding career and humanitarian accomplishment.